PLACES

Colette

PLACES

translated from the French by
DAVID LE VAY
and with a Foreword by
MARGARET CROSLAND

THE BOBBS-MERRILL COMPANY, INC.
Indianapolis / New York

Library of Congress Catalogue Card Number 70-163017

Translated from the French, and selected from
*Trois . . . Six . . . Neuf, En Pays Connu, Prisons et Paradis,
Paysages et Portraits, Journal Intermittent*

The Bobbs-Merrill Company, Inc.
A subsidiary of Howard W. Sams & Co., Inc.
Indianapolis / New York

Copyright © 1971 by the Bobbs-Merrill Company, Inc.
English translation © Copyright Peter Owen 1970

Trois . . . Six . . . Neuf . . . © Copyright by Editions Corrêa 1946.
En Pays Connu, Journal Intermittent © J. Ferenczi et Fils 1950.
Prisons et Paradis © J. Ferenczi et Fils 1932. *Paysages et Portraits*
© Flammarion 1958.

Printed in Great Britain

Foreword

Colette published over fifty books, but none called *Places*. Her deepest preoccupation was with the human heart, the animal mind, the birds, plants and trees that made up the earthly paradise. In one sense place was less important to her than the figures who peopled it, but her physical and emotional reactions to atmosphere were so strong that she invariably conveyed it with immediacy. She never wrote a description of a place as a literary set piece, as though she were looking at it through the lens of a camera with a list of fine phrases at her elbow. Description for her is inevitably mingled with living presence or the memory of it.

The delightful short book about moving house, *Three . . . Six . . . Nine . . .*, which opens this collection, mentions few facts and no relevant dates, but forms a kind of descant to the whole of her life. The rue Jacob: marriage to Willy, the writing of the 'Claudine' books published under his name. The rue de Villejust: flight into solitude. The chalet in Passy: marriage to Henri de Jouvenel and the birth of their daughter. Claridge's: life with Maurice Goudeket, who later became her third husband. The Palais-Royal: the years of legendary fame, which she could not have foreseen when this book was first published in France in 1944. This is the setting, already rich in historical associations,

5

which will frame her for posterity, and I will never forget my own visits to 9 rue de Beaujolais a few years before her death.

Much of Colette's favourite reading consisted of nineteenth century travel books, but on the whole she might well have agreed that travel narrows the mind. For her the contemplation of her own room or another woman's face could be a journey long enough, while the villages and towns of France, the *quartiers* of Paris, were worlds within themselves. Her writing about them is charged with colour, movement, humour or nostalgia. Although Colette travelled fairly widely—all round France when she was on the music-hall stage, and all round Europe as her fame spread and she was invited to lecture—she writes perhaps with most depth about her own country and more particularly about the places where she lived for a long time. Her birth-place was St Sauveur en Puisaye in Burgundy—Basse-Bourgogne to be precise—and it is not surprising therefore that she writes about the wine industry with such detailed knowledge.

As she grew older Colette moved about in more leisurely fashion, although throughout most winters she lived and worked intensively in Paris. She had a house in Brittany and later, near St Tropez, La Treille Muscate. She was commissioned by leading newspapers to write on such different themes as the maiden voyage of the *Normandie* and a sensational trial in Morocco. The trip to Scandinavia, described here, was made with Maurice Goudeket on the *Eros*, the beautiful yacht owned by Baron Henri de Rothschild.

The additional essays in this volume have been selected from *Prisons et Paradis* (1932), *En Pays Connu* (1949), *Journal Intermittent* (1949), *Paysages et Portraits* (1958). Short notes have been included in order to clarify references which might have seemed obscure to some British and American readers.

Margaret Crosland

Contents

Illustrations

Three . . . Six . . . Nine . . .

Only those, like me, who are sedentary by choice, may talk about moving house. What's more, they must have acquired, despite a strong attachment to the place they live in, the habit of leaving it. A settled fatalism, experience of both good luck and its opposite, these are the best, the most reliable agents of an exodus.

When a house has yielded all its essence, simple prudence counsels us to abandon it. It's a rind, a shell. We risk becoming its flesh, its kernel, of being consumed even unto death. Better to depart, to take the chance of at last finding a shelter that one can't exhaust; any peril is less than that of remaining.

In which faith, then, I have moved house, and not out of mere caprice. Often through force of circumstance, sometimes for moral hygiene. If the not so heavy chattels I drag around thereby acquire knocks and scars, so much the worse for them. Relatively frequent contact with the hampers for books and crockery, the used torn straw smelling of cellar and stable, the men shielded with triple-layered woollen aprons, expert at humping cupboards and sideboards on their backs with a single heave, with their snacks and their litre of purple wine—in short, my acquaintance with a fraternity that handles skilfully both the mirror-wardrobe and the little boat of spun glass is a useful one. And what better massage than an earthquake!

9

For those who see them only once in thirty years, the sight of the removal men, their appearance and behaviour, are forbidding. Enthusiasm is everything. After that comes a sort of delectation. This is sometimes born unexpectedly of the worst moment; I refer to the last stage of the move. The loaded vehicles move off : one is decent enough, fairly recently made, even motor-driven; the other two are miserable carts held together by ropes, with mournful animals in harness. You are left alone —you, I, us, the migrants—in the home you are deserting, among the wisps of straw, the bent nails, a picture-frame with only three sides. This stool lacking a seat? Leave it, the concierge can do what she likes with it. The walls, strangely resonant, echo your last words.

'Where's the cat? Under the bath. The dog's sneezing. No wonder, she's caught cold, everything has been left open since five this morning. But of course not, it's on account of the dust stirred up. This is the last time I'll choose such pale wallpaper, just look at the patches the sun has bleached. . . .

'You take the cat, give me the leash. Yes, but who's going to carry the *ex voto* from Notre Dame de Liesse?'

'Not me, Madame; if I should break it, Madame would let me know about it!'

'Downstairs, downstairs, it's freezing here. . . . Where shall we have lunch while we're waiting for the vans to arrive? Oh, there's plenty of time to worry about that. . . .'

Only the taxi-ride now links the two homes. We are shaken by the tremor of exile. The cat is hungry, the dog reserves its opinion. Tonight there begins a life in an unknown place, in cold beds that we shall make hurriedly.

Yes, but it is a new life, the sun will trace a new path on the wall, there will be new sounds at daybreak, a workroom facing south.

En route, en route! Our adventure, from one arrondissement to another, is worth the journey. 'Hold on to the cat, don't let go of the *ex voto*, fasten the old barometer round your neck with the leash, that will leave your hands free; put the bedspread over my shoulder while you pay the taxi and don't worry about anything else. . . . *En route*! But what can you have put in this bag that's so heavy?' None of us has slept for forty-eight hours. Never mind, fresh horizons are opening. . . . *En route*!

I have friends who pass as mentally normal, except that the idea of moving makes them screw up their eyes, shrug their shoulders, and put their hands over their ears, just as if they were on the pont des Arts on a very windy day. The bibliophiles suffer more in advance than others at the thought of moving. The collector of rare china suffers less because he knows—even should the house collapse, or the floor above accommodate a dancing school and an academy of singing—he knows that he will die rather than move.

There are those who have been on the edge of a decision for twenty years. 'This time Lucienne found something really charming; oh Lord, it wasn't one's dream, but still. . . . And then, after all, we let it slip. . . .' But these cases smell of masochism and I am not interested in them. I can recall only too well, and not without some self-disgust, when I nursed my incapacity, either to move or to settle into a new house, like an illness. There I was, among folded drowsy curtains, unopened packing-cases, a divan-bed, a rolled-up carpet from far away, and refused to take another step, with a constant desire to cry, as difficult to control as incontinence. I slept on the edge of the divan, I unrolled a corner of the carpet in the morning, I picked up a folded curtain that rattled its copper rings with the sound of an Egyptian dancing-girl. It was dark in the dining-room and the closets smelled of escaping gas.

One day my self-respect gained the ascendant. In one week the hovel, the apartment of 'after the crime', the poor divorcee's quarters, the incubator of anger, became a plain but welcoming 'little third floor'. The wash-stand which, when closed, offended the eye, disappeared like a bad dream, followed by its faithful blue enamel bucket. I sacrificed a little room to the demands of hygiene, installing the shower-hose and the verbena-rub, and adopted my first apartment. So it is that a new dog, who is not yet happy, resigns himself, fetches the ball, and picks the right cushion.

I referred earlier to those masochists who, while horrified by the very idea of moving, toy with that disaster as they might climb a tower to enjoy their dizziness from behind a railing. This perverted species begets a sedentary sub-species characterized by their visits to apartments to let. I once had occasion to accompany one of these specialists, to watch him measuring panels and exits in all directions, counting his steps and extending his arms : 'One metre sixty-five . . . I've a span of one metre sixty-five . . . the bookcase will just fit . . . but the dresser? The dresser will upset everything.'

For a long time he paced up and down the empty apartment and left in perplexity. Outside I noticed him wiping the sweat from his brow and asked him if he felt ill. 'Not at all,' he told me. 'It's just the thought that, if I moved, my beautiful soap-bubble service that I brought from Venice—and how difficult that was!—might end in bits and pieces in that market place, that . . . bazaar, that . . . I've no word for it. . . .' Thus, in a happy and remote era, this unworried Frenchman created purely imaginary risks to which he deliberately submitted. Such games never appealed to me; shams mean nothing to me. It was quite enough to come from a village, from a rural existence, where everyone was brought up in the ancestral house and garden and where moving house was barely conceivable, except that dying used to be called 'a removal between four boards'. My originally terrified idea of moving house slowly gave way, once I came to

Paris, to the idea of a free choice, the indulgence of whim, a
dream of pleasure. 'Why, I could, if I chose, live over a shop in
Paris, or in a deconsecrated chapel, or in a cottage at the edge
of the Bois.' In fact, I found myself stranded in a small third-
floor apartment in the rue Jacob, between two courtyards.

One has to be careful about living in a building situated
between two courtyards. I speak from experience. It's a difficult
kind of lodging. They come out of it best who make their home
their workroom, whatever their profession may be. In the contest
between work and an unfriendly apartment, it is nearly always
the work that wins, except possibly for the writer who is sensitive,
easily distressed by gloomy shadows, untimely shouts, the parrot's
cry and the litany of the radio. So let him not lightly settle in
between two courtyards, save at the risk of suffering unusual
noises, echoes, reflections of light, all factors that obsess the mind
and trouble it with illusion.

Marguerite Moreno,[1] who excels in imparting her strong
personality to an apartment, and even an hotel room, who is
capable of overcoming the inertia of a *studiotoutconfort*, of
reviving a mezzanine as passive as an old horse, even Moreno
packed her bags and fled from a modern apartment which
boasted, if I may so describe it, three very tall identical blocks
of oppressive grey, separated by courtyards. When I went to see
her I mistook the block and the courtyard and the staircase. I
have always been afraid of twins. She found words to reassure
me and to convince herself. 'You see, I've constant hot water,
and look how practical this bathroom is which can be washed
down, and look at all these built-in cupboards, and. . . .' At the
end of this demonstration and display she left the place and was
better off. That's the right way to behave, rather than wait
for such peremptory news, as it might be, of some nasty little
crime in the neighbourhood, a disease of long incubation, a
python coiled up under the pillow, misfortunes that entitle

one to exclaim: 'Ah! That's why I never felt happy in that house!'

In my first Parisian home I was like those adolescents that one overstrains because of an approaching examination. Too many things to learn, and chiefly that an open window reveals other perspectives than a grove or a clump of hydrangeas, admits familiar spirits other than the sounds of a garden, a dazed swallow, a wistaria tendril. What an eclipse of my original ideas! A single white feature: the porcelain dining-room stove, with its chimney moulded in the shape of a palm-tree trunk. I used to eat on my knees, rather than put up with the presence of the long-necked stove, a headless idol squatting in its rounded alcove.

As for the bedroom, I hardly ventured there save at night on account of the wardrobe mirror. Never since then have I come across a wardrobe with such a mournful mirror, a mirror crowned with a miserable little design in carved walnut and distorted right across its greyish surface by a fold like a moving wave that took me a long time to dare to remove. . . . Anyway, I was busy enough dealing with a gloomy alcove of a room both of whose doors functioned simultaneously and unexpectedly, opening to reveal a jumbled collection of empty trunks, a broken cot, tilted three-legged armchairs leaning watchfully over an upset pedestal table, which they had probably just assassinated. The deep alcove, the convulsive pair of doors, were of little avail against you, my twenty years, which had just lost, among other protectors, the tutelary wardrobe of the ancestral home, of rosewood lined with white thuja, impregnated with provincial order, sprigs of lavender and the dried petals of red roses.

Most of the houses along the rue Jacob, between the rue Bonaparte and the rue de Seine, date from the eighteenth century. I was much too young when I first settled in to give them their proper value. I found them sad and compared them to those girls of good family who devoted their entire virtue to staying virtuous. Some learned friend pointed out to me in vain that a President of Rosambo, the sculptor Pajou,[2] a king of Denmark, had lived and died in the rue Jacob; I listened absently and could not even bring myself to view the frivolous phantom of Adrienne Lecouvreur[3] with any awe. I found the thought of Mérimée,[4] my defunct neighbour, mc.e agreeable and I liked him all the more on discovering that he was no better housed during his lifetime than I.

I succeeded to a maniac guilty of having spent thirty years fixing thousands of little varicoloured lozenges on the ledges, doors, mouldings, fillets and frames of my first apartment. A dazzling heritage, dealt with by a good clean-up, that did not bother me for long. A lunatic leaves nothing of himself between the walls he has damaged in his lunacy for the simple reason that his mental dwelling is far removed from any real place. The only risk I incurred in the rue Jacob was the appeal of shadow, the seductive inducements of solitude. There I glimpsed the richness of all that is sombre, confined, conducive to static enjoyment; and, despite my twenty years, I desired only the briefest inrush of fresh air, a gust of spring hail rushing in through the open window, the vague odour of invisible lilacs from a nearby garden. Leaning far out over the window-ledge, I could glimpse only the top of a tree in this garden. I did not know that this focus of restless leaves marked the dwelling of Remy de Gourmont and the garden of his 'Amazon'. Much later I traversed the garden fence and visited the little temple dedicated by Adrienne Lecouvreur 'to Friendship'. Screened from the sun, this garden, even today, desires to nourish only ivy-smothered tombs, ancient pitted trees, and those aquatic plants that grow around the inside of wells.

I do not recall having done anything in the rue Jacob but wait. For the one who waits all other occupation is superfluous. Twenty

is an age when one can do without anything, save waiting for
what may happen. Everything is always about to come and I was
prone to take the most commonplace incidents for marvels and
omens. Such were the crossing from the left to the right bank and
the attainment of a painter's studio on the sixth floor where,
dazzled, I installed myself. What can I say of it now except that
its inhabitants were roasted alive in summer and frozen in
winter? Where did the painters paint in that period, when snobs
had acquired their proper studios in order to create cheaply,
without painting, something picturesque, with the basic furniture
of a refectory table, three goatskins made up to resemble bear,
and some antique chasuble? Quickly surfeited with the delights
of a glazed roof, cold northern light and violent swings of tem-
perature, I put to use a refuge on the landing. It was on this
wide top landing, remote from the general coming and going,
that I chose to sit, to install a table, an oil-lamp—and the cat,
who followed me. Perhaps he fled from the same torment as
I. . . .

This fine cat has left his name in literature : Kiki-la-Doucette.
Disdaining—and for good reason—the sexual passions, he spoke
very well, was an even better listener, could distinguish Vittel
from town water, and devoured *petits pois* leisurely one by one.
A spoonful of *petits pois* kept him busy for half an hour. Silent,
he and I on our landing, we seemed always to be waiting. Apart
from this cat, I recognized no *objet d'art* in this studio with its
three small adjacent rooms. A dining-room furnished by Dufayel,
all nails and leather, a bad upright piano, some imitation sunflowers, and wooden armchairs by Bing, each as luxurious as a
board. . . . Let us not disturb these marvels of nonentity, the
curtains, the lacquer, the portrait—mine—in Pre-Raphaelite
garments, by a young Turkish painter; in short this very Parisian
set-up. I was too provincial to dare to collect around me those
things that would have comfortingly recalled my beloved province.

Some five hundred yards from my second dwelling a third resting place awaited me. This was the scene of timid experiments, the witness of my first attempts to break out of my shell. Such attempts seem to make as little sense as the convulsions of an inhabited chrysalis. . . . But simplicity in daily life comes only slowly, and in stages. As far as interior decoration was concerned, I had only got so far as eccentricity which often suits the timid. Beneath this eccentricity they believe they can dissimulate their store of timorous goodwill and self-respect. What was the point of the painted wooden railing that I installed in the middle of the drawing-room, dividing it in two? A railing, and a massive one, like those surrounding suburban villas, a railing where young girls can fold their arms and dream, where children can sit astride and whistle. Absurd, almost intolerable, the white railing seemed to have been stranded there by a tidal wave, a precursor of de Chirico, a dream. . . .

'Hullo! What's that railing doing there?' people would say, coming in. I looked down my nose, bit a fingernail.

'It's just an idea. . . . Oh, I can see it's no good. I'll get rid of it.'

Neither of decorative nor practical use, the thing irretrievably spoiled the main room in everyone's opinion. That is, everyone's but mine, for I overlooked its inexplicable nature, its manner of ending abruptly in the middle of the marble hearth, blocking the table, taking the visitor's breath away. I promised to remove it, I didn't remove it. The new apartment wasn't too unattractive. It had been occupied by a very dusky Heredia,[5] unrelated to the poet of the same name. Behind the bourgeois facade—of two floors only—a peaceful, secluded garden and a small, squat house were silent.

It was all acceptable, a little sad, solid. So much so that I bought—as much for a symbol of a long stay as from any aspiration to elegance—an 'art noveau' table-lamp with a shade

sheathed in lilac flowers in pressed glass. I had seen a similar one
at my downstairs neighbour's, Prince Bibesco, one day when he'd
left his door ajar.

On the ground floor of this discreet house a three-year-old
child, the only child of the *concierges*, maintained an atmosphere
of combat and mordant humour for my pleasure and comfort.
Chubby, with curly fair hair, he inspired strangers with confidence, and they called him 'little angel'. But his parents regarded
him with consternation and he made his mother blush for the
bantering scorn he showed toward the female species. If she
whispered to a neighbour the 'little angel' would interrupt them :
'I know what you're talking about! You're talking about your
arse again!'

By dint of fox-cub cries and immoderate language he knew
how to teach his mother, when she came home from the market,
that 'it's shameful, really disgraceful, to leave a child of that age
all alone!' And he deliberately stayed awake part of the night.
Spying in the dark on the sounds and murmurs coming from his
parents' big bed, he would shout :

'Ah! Ah! I can hear you! I can hear you!'

At the age of four and a quarter he set out on an adventure,
taking a younger accomplice with him. They were caught in the
avenue Niel and the pioneer confessed that he had been planning
to plunder the Christmas toys counters in the shops of the
Economie Ménagère. This time he got a whipping, without
shrinking or complaining, and, retrousered, gave his own assess-
ment of the punishment :

'Well beaten,' he said.

Because I solemnly addressed him as 'Monsieur' he held me
in some esteem. He insisted on saying goodbye to me on his way
to exile, when his father, deciding that 'the lad had set everyone
by the ears long enough', sent him off to the country to stay with
a farmer cousin. Our poor superman returned a year later, rosy,

robust, and quite devoid of interest. He said: 'Good-day,
Madame. Thank you, Madame,' he recited stories. He had lost
his mystery. 'He's a good little lad now, you see', said his father
proudly. But his mother suddenly dissolved in tears, like a woman
in love who has been separated from her adored scoundrel. After
the little boy had paid me a visit my maid-of-all-work shook
her head and uttered a lugubrious prognosis on the subject: 'I
really do believe that that man's had it. . . .' The career of great
adventurers is soon over.

Some of my changes of residence assumed an explosive character.
I once compared them to those screen convulsions that flatten
a mountainside, excavate the site of a lake, empty a dam. . . .
But modesty has come with the years, and a better scale of
comparisons. Where I would have spoken of catastrophe I now
content myself with change. I had got as far as a railing, a puerile
enigma that I meant to remove from a drawing-room where it
was out of place. I could not find the time; everything to do with
it became insubstantial around me. At the seashore a patch of
mist sometimes surrounds us, holding us embedded in its opaque
strands, plastered fearful and blinded against a cliff face; then
the mist rises and exposes us, bare and damp, on a dazzling new
planet. The explosion very quietly fragmented a fragile dwelling,
its denizens, its climate of feeling, its furniture and trinkets. I had
to busy myself scraping together a little of the superfluous here,
a little of the necessary there. . . . To behave like a beachcomber
is an instinct with us.

Just as, later on, I knew how to haul out at the end of a
conger eel hook the debris deposited by the equinoctial swell—
a keg of rum, once, and a carton of chocolate ruined by the
salt, and a pretty little mahogany ladder—I knew, in the surge
of my modest personal cyclone, how to salvage the remnants of

the furniture. There are analogies between the one wreck and the other; the ladder, jetsam from some shattered luxury yacht, had sadly upset me; my collector's mania took a superstitious aversion to objects of furniture—lamps, armchairs, vases—that went in pairs. To the devil with twins and duplicates, a plague on everything coupled! I'd have gone as far, God forgive me, as to wish for a turtle-dove without a mate. Fortunately one gets over such childishness.

While awaiting an enduring lull, I could only abandon the walls I had made responsible, the rooms charged with meaning, and the four-footed chairs capable of browsing on the carpet during the night. *En route*! *En route* for the third time, holding by the reins a thinned-out, impoverished team. . . . Where is it, the roll-top desk that was too big for me? It was lost in transit. Farewell to the cane suite, imitation Louis XVI, to the dressing-table with its indescribable odour of bachelors and damp combs. . . . Three moves are as good as a fire, goes the proverb. What, only one fire for nine years of youth? That's a minimum of flames. At the end of this lease I departed, not sorry to leave the northern side of Paris, close to smoky Levallois, visible beyond the fortifications. These former strongholds, a hilly stretch planted with trees, cut by green ravines, and its idle sprawling population, gave birth in full measure to the literature of the period. . . .

This time I departed, but not without an objective and destination : I had a ground-floor flat in mind.

Formerly, a fair proportion of ground-floor apartments were reserved for love affairs, illicit or otherwise. Gloomy, the lights on in broad daylight, ill-ventilated; dark, with a spark of firelight glinting on a bottle or an ember; so confusingly dark that the host and his lady visitor might be glad to make a landfall on the dimly phosphorescent shore of the divan—so romance and reality depicted these bachelor quarters. Then a salutary promotion elevated these to the well-lit summits of modern blocks and the bachelor's establishment became a studio. Such a serious step dissipated many attractions.

What suits love, chaste work lays claim to. It, too, chooses to bolt the door, to light the lamp at high noon, to draw the curtains and establish silence. We are not attractive when we write. One pinches his cheek, another sucks his tongue, shrugs a shoulder; how many bite the inside of their cheek, hum as if at Mass, rub their heel on their shin? We are not—all of us—elegant; an old dressing-gown for preference and a rug over the knees, embroidered with holes by cigarette burns. . . . 'Quick, my slippers, I feel a poem coming on!' cried an otherwise charming and talented authoress. . . . The ground-floor flat conceals and encourages our tics, alters certain features of our character. Touchy about our neighbour, his piano, his child and his dog, we on the ground-floor tolerate the great booming of the *porte cochère*, which shakes our mattress and strikes a crystal note from the chandelier. When the cracked bell of the dustbins sounds it only half wakes us : 'It's only six o'clock!' and we go back to sleep.

Three, six, nine. . . . After my third move the thought of a change found me calm and seasoned. With unruffled countenance I contemplated the upsets that rubbed the cat up the wrong way (it wasn't, alas, still the same cat) and reduced my solitary maid to tears : 'Say what you like, Madame, our new place isn't central!'

Having foraged among my worldly goods, scanty enough, for my portrait by Ferdinand Humbert, a lithograph by Forain in which I had only one eye, the photograph of Lévy-Dhurmer's portrait of Renée Vivien,[6] a fish service that had never encountered, in my house, a turbot which was its match, a small gouache where my eighteen months shine in all their splendour, my bag of glass marbles (I still have them), some books and my lamp with its lilac flowers in mauve crystal, I departed. A little dwarf Japanese tree, not fond of being moved, died of this change of address.

In place of the house I used to live in, rue de Villejust, you will now find only a quite recently built and luxurious apartment block. In my time it was a house pleasing for its modest grace, its Batignolles charm. Once through the main gate you discovered that its shady courtyard communicated by a gate with the building that opened as No 23 on the avenue du Bois. The two shaded courtyards were as good as a garden : chestnut trees, borders of pink campions and blue forget-me-nots. Lanka, Robert d'Humières's white cat, used to come down from her Persian heaven to sit in the midst of the pink border, gazing at everything round about with her unnaturally blue eyes. Here she exposed her whiteness to the noisy admiration of the passers-by; a telegraph boy cried : 'A puff, a powder-puff!', the concierge facetiously called her Blackie and I murmured some white song for Lanka. It was all more than this creature of spun silver and sapphire could bear. She quivered all over at this too frank homage and rejoined, through an open window almost opposite mine, the master she loved single-heartedly.

I had never in my life lived alone. From the first night I spent in that ground-floor flat I forgot the key in the outside of the lock. This wasn't mere negligence, but confidence. I never trusted a roof as much as I did that one, which cost seventeen hundred francs a year. On the street side, one room was fully exposed to the sun. For the Leroy-Beaulieu mansion opposite, low and set back at the bottom of a courtyard, gave me all the benefit of the west. If I tell you that two other small rooms completed my domain I shall not have explained or pictured its charm and I should be very diffident in so doing today. Borne up at times by a novel gaiety, at others cradled in a boundless, unreasoning security, I only knew that I wanted to live and die there. In the mornings I heard the teams of horses, slowed down on the incline, slacken their pace under my window before turning the corner of the avenue, and the sun landed on my bed. When I think of the pitcher of cold water, of the pitcher of hot water by the side of the bath, I tell myself that such comfort sufficed for years. . . . A round piece of black English soap smelled of tar and roses and the sun danced in the water. . . .

Yes, I wanted to live and die there, roam the Bois in all weathers, open my window every day to watch the equestrians go by, and the equestriennes, fondle the ears of the horse that young Millevoye brought on to the pavement to say good-morning to me, exclaim at the ravishing mule ridden by Menabrea, admire the fine get-up of Iza de Comminges and Arthème Fayard's[7] smartness. Polaire[8] sometimes went by on her way to the stables of Mme Hensmann, who let out to her an astounding light bay mare, almost pink, whose black mane and tail nearly touched the ground. The early Amazons astride, of whom I was one, regarded this wasp on horseback with astonishment—her long skirt, her tormented smile, and the ribbon that bound her short hair on her neck and revealed—rare sight!—two perfect little ears. I wanted to ensure that I would enjoy this balcony for a long time, this modest vantage point above luxuriant movement, this calm at the heart of which I saw, astonished, shining and quivering from afar, I know not what tranquil flame that was meant for me, curled up in my hearth bordered by white marble. I wrote to Mme W., the invisible American proprietor, to inform her of my desire to grow old quietly in the rue de Villejust, to ask for a lease of twenty years, of thirty years.

She merely replied that the parent building was due for demolition and that fair compensation would be paid to all the tenants three months later. . . .

I did not resign myself lightly, for I knew the value of what I was about to lose. I had thought I was settled in and my stay, at best, would only last two and a half years. . . . The devil take Mme W. and her property speculations! We were a small group of tenants in her house, persons making little noise and possessing little money, content to breathe the air of the Bois, with its scent of catalpa in the spring, its yellow smell of fallen leaves in autumn. And we could all of us have wished that this American lady might have forgotten us there, with our wood-fire hearths, our bathtubs, our gas mantles and our pink-flowering chestnuts.

Moving out, settling in, I can boast of having learned ten kinds of wisdom, and as many of unreason. Although condemned, it was nonetheless this ground-floor apartment that I trusted—deaf to summer storms, sealed off from winter hurricanes—because of its illusory character as a place of asylum, with the hope of guarding secretly there, one day, a happiness that would at last be mine.

'Les Ternes! Now there's a district! Portuguese oysters are nine sous a dozen there, not the very biggest of course, butcher's meat is good value too. It's worth thinking about.'

Whose is the old voice that so admonished me? A voice, a face, almost forgotten. The voice of an old woman who taught me the recipe for *café au lait de concierge*, an appetising breakfast fit for a gourmand. . . . Does one still come across this species of old women, ending their lives in solitude, seeking grounds for living in sociability? This one, like so many others, lived to accost her fellow-creatures. Without removing her little cloche hat with its clusters of blackcurrants, she knew how to give a cacodylate

injection here, make an eggnog there, tell fortunes by cards somewhere else, roll cigarettes, accompany on the piano. . . . A gay
old lady, whose sad existence I could never contemplate without
a shudder. It was she who sought to console me for having to
leave the rue de Villejust. I refused to abandon my fourth apartment, I rejected the glowing future nourished on oysters at nine
sous the dozen, I wept in secret for my paradise at seventeen
hundred francs per annum, the neighbourhood of the Bois, of
Robert d'Humières and Renée Vivien, and even of a pension
restaurant hidden at the end of a lane of small gardens. After a
good plain dinner the family pension was transformed into a
small gambling den, where louis and banknotes mingled in the
kitty. . . . This poker was not for me but sometimes, out of
condescension and for want of anything better to do, the *patronne*
initiated me into bezique.

She played every hand at arm's length, her exceptional cor-
pulence keeping her well away from the table. Never did a quiet
inn shelter a more frenzied game. Four poker players in particular, a woman and three men, used to arrive above five in the
afternoon, dined meagrely, stayed the night, had some chocolate
at two in the morning and onion soup at eight, washed their
hands, drank a whisky and soda at eleven, went home around
midday for a bath and siesta, and then began all over again.
Their enjoyment showed every mark of resignation and they
exchanged only the most essential comments. The winner never
seemed any more cheerful than the losers. I neither knew nor
liked them. But, seeing them so committed to their game and
their silence, I believed them full of mortification because they
did not laugh, and mysterious because they were silent. Were
they worth the ten lines I've given them? Yes, if you concede
that these recollections, which exclude the leading parts, may
include, in settings that collapse like card houses, the walkers-on,
the figures stuck on the back-cloth, the little people who have

acted dumbly or uttered tonelessly three sometimes sibylline
words.

'You know, it's nicer at les Ternes than here,' insinuated the
old lady. 'They're building all the time. You can get marvellous
places now at unbeatable prices—for two thousand five hundred
or two thousand eight hundred francs.'

I had never had much liking for princely panelling. Les Ternes
. . . why not the Grand-Montrouge? Discouraged, I faced the
inevitable. That's how I ended up in an intermediate zone, as
much péreirienne as ternoise, named after an heroic sergeant,
a canonized Sénoch, a Bayen dominated by the château des
Ternes.

'Like this,' pursued the wise old voice, 'with the trams, you
can actually be at the Madeleine in twenty minutes.'
Such an argument left me speechless, I who never went to
the Madeleine except to guzzle at Hédiard's.
The gradual encroachment on private parks in Paris is almost
complete. Around 1908 a delightful garden existed alongside the
château des Ternes. The wild violets in the spring, under the
trees! A street destroyed it. Then, after that, twenty apartment
blocks were built on the rest of the park. With the trees they
brought down nests, and still more nests. It was in the midst of
all this devastation that I settled in myself in a barely-finished
ground-floor apartment. The architect responsible remarked to
me that, by lowering one of the three front windows to pavement
level, I could have a private entrance. It should be mentioned
that, at this time, the vogue for the artist's studio was giving way

to one for a ground-floor flat with its own entrance. More pleasing to one's vanity than useful. 'It's perfect, my dear, you won't have to go past the concierge's lodge! And it's marvellous for the dogs!' I soon became surfeited with the pleasure of putting my dog out ... to dream on the pavement without having to go past the concierge. Besides, the bulldog made it a point of honour to exit by jumping through the window and to return the same way. It was the cat who made most use of the privileged entry. She cemented relations in the district, was on familiar terms with three little black dogs, all harnessed with ribbons and bells as if for a circus. She sometimes cuffed them and sometimes welcomed them in an affected fashion, sitting up like a rabbit with forepaws raised. In the event, both cuffs and charm were to no purpose; the schipperkes never understood anything about the feline race.

Our ideal dwelling-place always remains more or less imaginary. My changes of home were not so much in pursuit of the realization of a dream as, each time, in the renunciation of it. The house where one was born, however dearly loved, never exists in complete reality since we see it with the eyes of childhood, vast and distorted. If I could paint I should have tried to paint the house I wanted to inhabit. Gradually elaborated from random enthusiasms, it had the myriad facets of a fly's eye. Even today I can't count on refraining from adding to its different aspects. One wall is covered by a double myrtle, flower-starred as the firmament. If it's still alive it continues to flower madly, and I know that, on moonless summer nights, its whiteness lightens a grey granite wall which it covers up to the roof. Another favourite facade possesses a cloak of dense vines, dense and cold, defying the heavy rains. Yet another facade has beside it a bountiful little spring, a kind of font which pours out over the centuries an inexhaustible abundance of water in the shape of a liquid drapery with a frayed-out edge, a naiad's tunic suspended for eternity from the same side of the well-head. I found this once only; but I possess and carry the spring with me everywhere.

I have also plastered with intangible pink daub a south-facing wall, dry and creviced, smelling of warm bread and rosemary, flaking so as to provide a hundred little lairs for the flat lizards. . . . But perfection exists only in that which is outside human dimensions : the entry to my ideal home I borrowed, once, from the sea. I reached it along a path, real enough, that cut across a sea-meadow, bare and salty, a well-trodden path kept open by the feet of men and sheep, bordered by nightshade, privet, honey-suckle, tamarisks stunted by the Breton wind. In Brittany the summer air is blue in the mornings and gains its odour from the wild white roses that spring stalkless, open on the short grass like the roses of Persian carpets. Along this real pathway I could plunder everything, from flowers to blackberries. My productive dream began with nothing more than an excavation of rock just by the seashore. Every tide filled and populated it; it remained full during low tide. The limpidity of the water, its blue-green colour, the magic greenish-blue of the seaweed, carried to ex-tremes the shadowy transparency, the deceptive limitlessness, of the cavity. As soon as I cast my shadow on its mirror a swarm of shrimps took flight on its pink and green bottom, to gain the protection of its most indented wall, fronded with vegetation. In July the midday sun stabbed the still water almost vertically and, in imagination, I descended the seaweed stairs across seawrack and fucus, ferns and purple mosses. A shoal of minute fish, two black streamlined fingers of a little groping octopus, a crowd of shrimps, the palpitation of a sentient tuft, pink as the dawn, cradled by the clear luminous water. So much life! Three little blue and gold gurnards, spiny at head and gills, darted from seaweed to seaweed like hummingbirds. A shrimp at the top-most ˙branch of a fucus played the solitary nightingale of this Eden.

The bottom of my well opened into a grotto barely a foot high. Under its vault, dully gleaming with every possible hue of green and blue, there dreamed a visitor, not always the same. I've seen a crab there in military blue and red; an octopus who shrank up as soon as he felt my gaze; a conger-eel, all its teeth displayed; a big gurnard with low forehead. . . . Whatever the creature, it was securely protected in its niche, sheltered by the overhang from light and shade, and I made one of those vows that one admits to no one : 'If only I could live in a den like that! If only I might emerge as if it were giving me birth! If I could but return to it as if to a time before my birth!'

A naïve woman of my acquaintance persisted for thirty years in turning up the left brim of all her hats under an ostrich feather, imagining that in this way she was the living image of La Grande Mademoiselle.[9] So there is no need for surprise if, by using an olive-green velvet wallpaper, I attempted to transform a ground-floor apartment in les Ternes into a marine grotto. Save for that grotto, I've found nowhere that seemed fit to live in for any time, except a wren's nest that I picked up, empty. Its precisely rounded interior, perforated with a minute entry hole, smelling of hay and wild thyme sprigs, was studded with fine grasses and strands of horsehair. I stayed in that nest for a period of some weeks, then abandoned it. It was not the least painful of my removals.

Potted ferns, meadow-sweet, dwarf rose-trees, the resigned flowerless vegetation we undiscriminatingly label 'green plants', a few clumps of hairy primulas and lobelia and calceolaria—nor did I forget, in the spring, my thirty square centimetres of forget-me-nots and those small rectangular containers shaped like apple-tarts, stuffed with red daisies—I furnished my entrance-hall with these in the vain hope that it would remind me of my

marine grotto. But my garden gently insisted on turning yellow
and then dying. And as for me. . . .

But I didn't try to run away. A certain degree of inertia isn't
a bad thing, as long as it doesn't lead to despair. Polaire was
accustomed to placing herself in God's hands and expressed her
humble faith in ingenuous words: 'It's just when one is a hundred
feet deep . . . that, suddenly, something comes and pulls you out.'
She was not mistaken; a crowning mercy at last rescued her from
a hundred feet of painful living.

The ever-unexpected breeze, the burning oxygen that gives
women their life and colour, buffeted my cloistered little gardens,
quickened my olive-green refuge; the telephone crackled day and
night. Keen happiness and stunning misfortune menaced me
simultaneously. I hesitated under their impact, I was so anxious
to show the same respect and interest towards the one as the
other. The period of my extraordinary homes dates from this
extraordinary season of the heart.

And, to begin with, I agreed to move to the sixteenth
arrondissement to live in one of the 'Swiss chalets' bestowed by
the first half of the nineteenth century on the village of Passy.
Flimsily built, guaranteed for fifty years, a good many lasted for
a century. I had already come across one of these in the rue des
Perchamps, like a bungalow perched on slender wooden stilts.
It presided over a garden of three thousand metres, abandoned
to ancient trees, rose briars, filbert-bushes and emancipated
cats. . . .

The chalet that yawned open for me as a kind of trap was,
on its modest scale, very similar to a piece of Swiss stage-setting.
It possessed the fragility and sound alpine style of a piece of
scenery, the porch-roof pierced with trefoils, the balconies and
timbering on the surface of the brickwork. The virgin vine took
care of the rest, in festoons and garlands. This chalet occupied
the end of a garden surrounded by gardens and its Helvetic

romanticism was enhanced by legend : the small courtyard owed its *porte cochère* and its lock, both in massive metalwork, to a jealous painter infatuated with his model.

The first time I passed through the heavy gateway was on a luminous night in the month of June, with acacia clusters and red lamps masked behind curtains. An enormous full moon, poised on the angle of the roof, seemed about to sing. Walls hid the surrounding gardens. I halted at the border of this enticement, this excessive charm, this ambush. Perhaps there was still time to retrace my steps. But already my host appeared in front of me. . . .

Within the chalet, poverty and excess conspired to maintain my enchantment. The bathroom was installed in a shed and had only been thought of for the use of the dogs of the household. The former painter's studio, at a distance from the chalet, was decorated with Louis XV panelling but its ceiling let in the rain. A gallery bookshelf contained little but Latin authors bound in calf and a few odd volumes of memoirs—the literary provender, in fact, of those provincial châteaux where one goes to bed at nine o'clock. . . . Jealous of the dogs, I too demanded a bathroom. Imprudent wish! As soon as the artisans got to work on it the chalet gave way here and there, fulfilling its role as a worn-out stage-set, its comedy of fantasy and illusion. The least of the plumber's activities made urgent demands on the builder; the humidity and moonlight of Perrault's tales cut off the electricity. At the autumnal equinox great sheets of the trefoil-pierced porch flew away with the leaves and roof-slates. Then I used to light a wood fire and work on, waiting for the end of the gusts, the end of the bad weather, the end of a comfortable doze. No house ever advised me so loyally to wait. Someone—perhaps the beautiful cloistered model—must have had to wait at length in the same room, before a wood fire, and I did my sentry duty patiently.

The birth of a child,[10] the first two years of the Great War, letters that failed to arrive—whatever I waited for within the chalet's crumbling walls was of no importance, since, when barely past its peak, the feeling of vigil was spontaneously reborn. In the vigil of the night, the hand-rail was the height of one's folded arms. During the daily vigil everything came to my aid : the still severity of the cat, the hesitancy of the drops of rain, the yawning of the dogs. . . . Suddenly a letter dropped into the letter-box, the dogs bounded as if called, and the whole house and I also ceased waiting, fearing, imagining.

I owe a great deal to the chalet at Passy. Under its balconies and its trefoils I led a really feminine life, marked by everyday curable sorrows, revolts, laughter and cowardice. It was there I acquired the taste for decorating and destroying. There I worked, harried by the need for money. There I spent hours of idleness. An innocent and flower-decked cottage in good weather, the long nights and lowering skies changed the chalet into a little 'scene of the crime', aided by the gaping darkness of the shed, some walled-up windows, and a store-room reeking of rotten carrots.

Never did a small house in process of self-destruction have such persistent vitality and express it so variously. The animals prospered and multiplied there, the cats flared their nostrils at the scent of the yellow rat, and the yellow rats feared only the owls. I owned an acrobatic squirrel, two snakes, one a viper with a pink belly, two green lizards. The first weeks of a new-born girl were warmed by the July sun . . . worm-eaten, condemned, even its framework spongy, the chalet spoke only of the future and of growth. But. . . .

But one day, running indoors from a summer storm, I climbed to the first floor to change my clothes. 'What a strange optical illusion,' I said to myself. 'I'd swear that that great silver shower is slanting across the bathroom.' What had happened was that a corner of the chalet had just fallen into the bottom of the garden. The thin bricks and slender beams had made less noise in their fall than the thunder. And as the Great War was not yet over, the tenants and the proprietors often competed in destitution. The owner of the Swiss chalet, short of cash for urgent repairs, revoked the lease and . . . I set off in search of another roof, for lack of another chalet. Not that the Swiss variety is completely extinct. My own, cut across by a roadway, made a good heap of rubble eventually. I know of one or two of them, surrounded and threatened by concrete, that still hold out. Right up to the end they preserve their flora and fauna, their ambiguous facade— half Eden, half the house of a murderer's victim—with their charming spread of clematis at the front.

Dispossessed once more, did I lose heart? Not at all. One loses courage and patience when one moves only twice in a half-century. But migrants of my type, untrammelled by concealed lighting, decorative paintings or chandeliers, can get settled in within forty-eight hours. More than once I've mystified friends, gallant neurotics whom my own removals so filled with horror as to prevent them from sleeping, and who came to get a thrill from seeing me in my new home, all boxes of books, jumbled furniture, and my fragrant collaborators, the removal men.

'Ah! What a nightmare!' they would sigh.

'Quite. Go away. Come back tonight about six. Will you help me?'

'Oh! Of course, you poor dear! Ah, what. . . .'

'You've said that once. Until this evening.'

On the stroke of six, carpets unrolled, three pairs of curtains hung, the lamps plugged into their sockets, I pretended to be reading or working, as if I'd been there for ten years. The bulldog and the cat lent their malicious aid, the one quietly at her toilet, the other snoring in her basket. The other little minor spirits, such as armchairs and glass balls of paper-weights, played their parts to the life in a touching tableau of old and lasting cosiness. . . . How my friends laughed. . . .

I needed a seventh home, that is, a small dwelling to satisfy the taste, acquired in the chalet, for a miniature enclosed universe where I should not encounter 'people' on the stairs. I had to have one, no matter where. A low house in Auteuil attracted me. It concealed a garden and in front there was a green confusion, a copse, a luxuriant ravine despoiled by the fortifications. Beyond the ravine was the Bois. . . . What, would the Bois belong to me too? I rang.

A pretty, made-up young woman opened the door and said, in uncertain tones, 'I'll go and see.' She left me in a drawing-room which seemed empty, though furnished, and which ignored me. Agile in her girl's skirt, the young woman returned, leading a person in a wrapper of grey and black flannelette with ban-daged eyes. The bandage pushed up over her forehead a mop of thick iron-grey hair, wiry and uneven, and when she walked she groped in the air with two little wrinkled, touchingly fragile hands. She said :

'Madame. . . . Whom have I the pleasure . . .?'

I suppressed an exclamation of surprise, for I recognized simultaneously the sound of her voice, the small hands, the chin barely touched by age, the well-spaced teeth, and I said : 'Eve. . . .'

It was Lavallière[11] before me, almost blinded in an accident, plunged in the dark abyss, not made up, curls unhennaed, lost in a poor old gentleman's dressing-gown, too long and too wide, the sort of chance garment one flings round those rescued from a fire or from drowning. . . . As soon as I identified myself she gave an exclamation and hurriedly explained that she was near-ing the end of her cure. Braced by the powerful instinct of coquetry, she flapped about in that vast and deplorable garment like a swallow caught up in a curtain, so that I might conjure up her slenderness, vivacity and gracefulness. She told me about her new *entresol* : 'Champs-Elysées, above Panhard's, my dear!'

She insisted on accompanying me as far as the front door and said, holding out her little blind hand, 'Ah, it's raining! Again', and threw me a kiss with that hand that missed its mark. . . .

It might perhaps have been as well if this had been my last glimpse of Lavallière, injured for a time in her finest feature— her mobile, slightly divergent, luminous eyes. By good luck she recovered. I saw her again, before what was referred to as her conversion, in that same small house on the outer boulevard that I was to inhabit for a few years.

One morning I met her on the fortifications of Auteuil, irregular shrubberies where acacia and maple flourished. Lavallière was playing with her dog. I think she was delighted, that morning, to show me that it was all over with bandaging, flannel dressing-gown, and ripe age. She wore a jersey costume of a light cigar colour over a soft blue sweater, a little masculine Havana felt hat beneath whose brim her eyes, restored, shone with youth. Apart from her face, neck and hands, her slender, aggressive body remained entirely and indisputably young. She spoke to me passionately and repeatedly about the theatre. Suddenly she broke off, pulled up her sweater over her transparent chemise, and exhibited the torso of a young girl, undisguised by girdle or brassiere. She pressed one hand on her small, well-placed breast and cried in a despairing, indescribably reproachful, voice : 'You see, it's real enough, all this! It's really me! I exist!'

I succeeded her in the house on the boulevard while she was installing herself at the Champs-Elysées, and she invited me to dinner in her new *entresol*. A young interior decorator had decided that the dining-table should be supported by huge caryatids, massive in carved wood, placed so that the guests had no choice except to bruise their knee-caps or keep well away from their plates. In order to miss none of the sunshine Lavallière decided to have her coffee seated on the floor, arms linked round her knees. Thus she was constrained to lift her eyes towards us, eyes sometimes gay, sometimes full of obscure entreaty. Her restless hand often touched and disarranged her hair, black once more, which displayed an artificial, opaque, purplish tinge in the sun's rays.

So, after her, I lived in her house. Because the times were difficult—the war dragged on—I respected what she'd left behind. An ochre and black batik remained on the bedroom walls, another voluminous white and red batik draped three windows. Linoleum imitated black and white tiling. A very low divan bed, covered with tarnished gold lace, was offensive to the touch and, on damp days, to the nostrils. I couldn't see any object of luxury or decent solidity, a carpet of reasonable quality, a firm elastic mattress, a well-painted surface. Did Lavallière possess, at that time, any of those jewels an actress may genuinely wear in the midst of her fictions, the heavy solitaire casting its gleams over every gesture of a drama and hypnotizing the spectator? Probably, but I'm not sure. Her girlish figure, so graceful on the stage, hampered her prospects as an actress, as she was well aware.

'Cheirel can play a mother,' she said, 'Lender can play a mother, but not I. When I'm sixty everyone will laugh if I try to play a mother. So what? Must I die?'

She did die, in effect, to the world and to the stage.

The last time I saw her, at some mutual friends, her entrance made us glow with pleasure. A couturier had designed for her a sort of schoolgirl's smock in black satin, with a low gathered waist and long sleeves; the yoke came up to her neck and widened into a ruff, which was also gathered. The childish feet, the legs

Paris loved, were delightfully visible beneath the short apron-dress, whose pink lining peeped out beneath the hem of the skirt, at the back of the ruff, at the ends of the sleeves, and on the inside of the pockets, also gathered, in which Eve Lavallière stuck her small wrists like an urchin. Sad and gay, old and young, that evening she was sometimes twenty, sometimes sixty. I happened to be about when she was leaving and uttered a sincere commonplace:

'You're ravishing in that dress . . . those little pockets with their pink lining are absolutely charming!'

'Yes,' she said. 'And then, they come in useful. . . .'

Bravely she held out her delicate hands, all fragile ossicles, tendons, shadowy veins ramifying and distended under the irremediably wrinkled skin. . . .

'. . . to hide these,' she finished.

She leaped on tiptoe, did a ballerina's pirouette, and disappeared.

The private mansion that is fond of a family is marked by a singular malleability. Most of our Parisian houses are disappearing, either with the passing of time or by the pickaxe. Their construction was motivated by an intransigent egoism that was the egoism of the couple. 'A nest, a real nest!' they cried. But they were nests where few eggs were laid. After a trial, its occupants perceived that the nest for two would have better suited a spinster or a bachelor as soon as 'the question of children' came up. For the question of children simultaneously posed the question of the children's room. The limitations of housing make for miserly bellies. Here and there one comes across houses favourable to reproduction, their vocation revealed by use. They overflow from good nature, one might almost say from elasticity. A space is created for an unforeseen little bed here, a window opened there. A junk room is promoted to the status of housing and incubating a white cocoon bedded in its cradle. The pre-destined house seems to spread out like a hen over her chicks.

But it was not like that with Lavallière's former house. This small mansion had shrivelled up, doubtless from lack of love. A tormented soul, drawn towards faith but eager to continue to shine, desperate at inhabiting an ageing body, frank and child-like, had pined between its walls. But it was in no way hostile towards me. I sensed its fragility and protected to the best of my ability the dwelling that gave me so little protection. At the first sound of a night alert, from 1915 to 1918, I opened the windows—it was important to save the glass—and went back to bed. All around me in my loneliness—my husband at the Eastern Front, my child in the country—the house resounded like an empty barrel when the bombers passed overhead. I admired my elderly cat, a large blue Persian, for the impression she gave of seeing them and following their flight through the ceiling. She did not seem at all distressed; the added noise merely made her turn her gaze. Apart from the affection she had for me, this cat of great character only entered into friendly relations with Auteuillois of good standing, chosen from those who'd say: 'I'm off to Paris, is there anything you want doing?' They patted their pockets before leaving, checked their keys and purse, asked themselves: 'Let's see, shall I take the No 16 or the métro?'

My neighbours loved all animals, hairy and feathered alike. The cat visited them by bounding over the wall—a long, blue, gliding stream. The servant with me at that time, tossed her head jealously: 'One of the neighbours' sons takes our cat onto his bed. The other son sketches her. And they've a friend who makes a photo from it for postcards! We can't do anything about it.'

Though the small mansion became bereft of its master, the event mattered little to the memories that trace their nomad paths in thresholds and vestibules, the hidden guiding influence, the barely decipherable activity of chance, the influence exerted on me by precursors who, in each new dwelling-place, bedded their insomnia beside a wall, loitered by a window with their face behind a curtain. What I'd spent myself for three years to give to it, the little house dissipated in a month. The ground floor returned to its gloomy dampness, the drawing-room expelled me to the first floor, whither I carried on a plate the solitary female's snack. In the hall my bicycle took the place of a coat-rack. Everything became pared down again to sober essentials save for the garden, reserved for the tits and nightingales of its wall full of nests, rose-trees, heliotrope and a long wistaria. A charming little garden; but I was no longer capable of believing that existence can be led beneath an arbour or that a pergola makes up for the majority of evils. I was able to contemplate my own errors as lucidly as those of others.

What then? Was the pleasant little house losing its soul so quickly? But was it one of those one finds attractive? No, it is we who are attractive. Once we have departed, removed ourselves, once the great tidal wave of love has withdrawn to the bounds of the horizon, the habitation corresponds in value to certain seaside villas : at high tide they are irresistible, but low tide uncovers a muddy expanse stinking of rotting mussels. The small Lavallière house lacked what had sustained the Swiss chalet against woodworm and the elements : a secret, a lyrical bad style, a spell—in short a poem.

But where could I go, once more? The aftermath of war stripped Paris of all its To Let notices. It was then that, unforeseen, unsought, feared even, a rainbow arc encircled my perplexity : the arch of an *entresol* window above the gardens of the Palais Royal.

Ancient and historic sites are associated with enduring legends, the most tenacious of which are rarely to their credit. The Palais

Royal is remembered for its bad reputation and not because it cradled the Revolution. It is a fact that Paris is not very familiar with Paris. Thus, the gardens are known and frequented only by riverside dwellers and immediate neighbours. Then again, the latter need to be endowed with a small child or a dog—the one doesn't exclude the other—for whom hygiene demands a reliable resort. The length and breadth of the garden cannot really be appreciated if it is only used as a short cut. Chance and idleness are the chief guides of the passer-by, who stops to exclaim 'How beautiful this is!' This masterpiece, hastily erected in four years, tottering nearly everywhere, has no detractors. Its medium regular height permits the low descent of a great ceiling of the Parisian sky, the dawn rises rapidly above its roofs, the setting sun has time to redden them and the flowers last there into late autumn. Paris is unaware of all else, the fact, for instance, that a particular magic attaches to the *entresols* of the Palais Royal. Nowhere else do the advantages of a pleasant life so insolently defy the normal conditions of existence. On the Palais's upper floors the satisfaction of overlooking the hedges and lawns, of gazing up at the changing sky, breathing the odour of flower-beds after rain, is self-evident. But the *entresols*? Am I the only one who defends or will defend these lairs huddled under the arches, squeezed between the first floor and the shops beneath?

A modest rent, a ceiling I can touch with my hand—two metres, twenty-five decimetres—an extent in length of fourteen metres and seventy decimetres, to be disposed of as I wished: these were the inducements chance offered me. Me, who charged head down through leases and contracts. This residence was so strange that I hesitated before my apartment at No 9. However, one day all was signed and sealed and I dived into the tunnel, the socket, the drain-pipe, the drawer. . . .

'Take care not to jump for joy there,' advised a wit, 'or you'll fracture your skull.'

'I'll jump for joy,' I replied, 'when Quinson, who's director of the theatre next door, leases me the first-floor apartment immediately overhead.'

But I ceased to envy that sunny floor, I took such a liking to the sombre level where I could hang curtains and pictures without need of a step-ladder, merely by rising on tiptoe. In broad daylight the paving of the arcades and the sun in the garden threw a footlight glow on the ceiling. No sky to be seen save—on the Beaujolais aspect—the flow of clouds that stream over the rue Vivienne. On the garden side the arch of my windows exactly matched the curves of the arcades, and in the evenings each arcade was lit by a large oil-lamp. Beyond the two arches I could see the tree trunks of the arbour, the quivering of whipped-up water in the great fountain. As for the ceiling of the arcades and the supports of the lanterns, these belonged, then and now, to the sparrows and the courting pigeons.

I did not include in the attractions of my cloister an old Colonial Bureau that used to disfigure the Chartres and Orléans galleries. Its crumbling glass roof hardly sheltered the pedestrian and its exotic treasures comprised faded butterflies from Oceania, specimens of hardwood, photographs of palm-groves, Tahitian coconut-groves and Marquesan waterfalls. None of this, abolished these past ten years, was worth preserving except in memory, which is uncomplainingly stuffed with dead show-cases and faded coleoptera. But my first morning at the Palais Royal, eyes still closed, gave the illusion of a fine day in the country; for a gardener's rake worked to and fro beneath my window, the wind blew from west to east in the leaves, and a liquid gurgling rose and fell in the pigeons' sonorous throats.

Under my window there passed and repassed the users of the Perron passage, who, it seemed to me, traversed my strange apartment from one end to the other.

But I wasn't bothered by these unseen individuals, rather the contrary. I soon got to like, too, the ship's throbbing imitated by a printing press beneath me. How calm the nights were, protected by police in couples! A love-sick cat sang, then stopped singing to sharpen its claws on the bark of an elm. Night sounds filtered through the two open ends of my tunnel, skirted my bed, and made their exit by gently jumping through the window opposite. . . .

Repose of mind and body is not dependent on silence. I've slept most soundly at night on the Canebière,[12] that torrent by night and day. My 'tunnel', haunted by footfalls and voices, cradled a unique peace. The cat and dog, too, felt they could enjoy reasonable quiet there. They recorded in their accurate memories the eleven o'clock dog, the noonday child, the ball-players at two, the *Intransigeant*, right up to the night watchman who brought down the plaster from our ceiling when he slammed the gates.

Both of them had certainly approved of my former dwellings. Both of them—and their defunct predecessors—were of the tribe who like us and avow that where we are is home, temple and place of refuge. Cat and dog were particularly taken with the new semi-basement, like living in a drawer, rich in shadow to which, even in broad daylight, artificial lighting lent the bright colours of a minor nocturnal enchantment. Nowhere had the cat been more given to racing up and down—it wasn't possible cross-ways—chasing after the ghosts, themselves, I think, longitudinal, that it pursued for fourteen metres and seventy decimetres, and fourteen metres and seventy decimetres, and again fourteen metres and seventy. . . . Nowhere had the rounded skull of my bulldog been so crammed with documents, proper names, varied sounds and images which it registered in bulldog fashion during that animal reverie that we inaccurately call sleep.

She adored words. But I can hardly say that all the words she registered, from 'raspberry' to 'right' and 'left' were useless, for this would overlook the distinction she taught herself to make between 'wicker chair' and 'little red armchair'. And after all, it was her affair and not mine.

A gambling-den, worse maybe? I don't really know, they're just stories I tell myself. It may be that the *entresol* where I hollowed out my nest had in fact been the dwelling, the observation post, of those ladies of pleasure, who—because of their hiding-place and its arched window—were called beavers or semi-beavers, depending on whether their means and the profits of their industry made them tenants of a whole or half a window.

So I dug myself in at the base of one of those buildings with similar repetitive facades where one is unaware, seeing them only from the gardens, how narrow they are and how full of inconveniences and attractions. Jerry-built, they were repaired merely by strengthening the walls with daub and sealing-wax. 'My floor is warped,' I said to M. Ventre, similarly besotted with the regal undermined building.

'No, Madame, it's not warped, it's sinking!'

'Where to?'

'Ah, Madame, to wherever it may please God.'

Charming illusion as it was in my *entresol*, I had no yearnings for the ground-floor. The forest of sturdy columns at the corners of the Palais will inspire confidence for a long time to come; not everyone need know that the core of these great pillars is made of decaying wood. And I proceeded from discovery to discovery. I rubbed elbows with strange orthopaedic appliances and camouflaged goldbeater's skin, I loitered before the illustrated covers on display at the latest promiscuous bookshops: *The Empress of Patent Leather, Spurs and Riding-whips. ...* I encountered, at their respective times, elderly ladies, officially destitute, men who appeared respectable but who, as they passed, made mothers hurriedly grasp their playing children. . . .

Paris barely knows Paris; and it did not take me long to persuade myself that these encounters were endowed with a particular charm, that everything in that garden was consecrated to goodwill and mutual helpfulness, courtesy and neighbourly pleasures. You consider me mistaken? Still, envy me! For why shouldn't I have given as much credence to innocence as to bad repute? All my recollections of delightful dwellings paled before the welcome accorded me by this domain. Close by were les Halles, well-stocked in 1930, streets dotted with decent restaurants, accessible theatres, the park-like Tuileries, the *quais* and the islands—I could go on for ever about all that began to brighten my life. On moonlit nights the Carrousel was silvered, the gardens blue and black, and magic turned every cat grey. A daughter of my cat, very beautiful and somewhat stupid, went down and paraded between the columns so like the other columns, the shadows of the arcades ranged behind the arcades, until she began to run round the garden twenty times, crying: 'Help! I'm shut out!'

Authentic nights, deceptive days, a lamp on my work-table at high noon, afternoons under a green lamp-shade. . . . I forgot that I was living removed from the sun's blessing, satisfied with mere reflections. If, in my second winter there, I had bronchitis badly, the cat, despite her midday promenades in scarlet harness, developed pulmonary congestion. Together we recovered, together we enjoyed the return of the fine weather—reflected, ricocheted, indirect.

But the following winter the bronchitis was punctually at its post in my bronchi, where it created a noise like the rustling of paper petticoats. It brought, too, its crystalline company of cupping-glasses and its little febrile attendant, the pleuritic focus. . . . One rarely cracks up without some satisfaction and how delightful diminished reality can be! Outside, the clock of the Bibliothèque Nationale ticked away the hours. A milk-cart, briskly moving over the asphalt paving, seemed to lose its vehicle and become reduced to the horse alone. . . .

'It's my opinion you've fooled around in this cave long enough,' my doctor said to me.

'But,' I objected, 'I'm waiting for the apartment above. Gustave Quinson has promised it to me. . . . In two and a half years, as soon as his lease. . . .'

'Two and a half years! You're not serious!'

The word 'removal' fell on my accustomed ear. Other words followed, advance descriptions of a high, airy, bright situation. In advance I shut my eyes to it, just as when the mistral inflicts on Provence an excess of light, wind and flying sand. However, I reckoned what I should have to lose—the Galerie Vivienne, for instance, with its two hidden interior lanes where Falstaff would be unable to pass; their gates wafting darkness, the foot-betraying thresholds. To think that gas and electricity have still not rejuvenated their innocent decrepitude . . . and Véro-Dodat, ceiled with Empire paintings . . . and all those *trages*, as we say in Franche-Comté, labelled Pothier passage, Beaujolais passage, and even Public passage. . . .

And the crooked exit that led, between two fine pavilions of a discreditable past, to a 'clinic for cravats'! Had I sufficiently admired that period staircase, with its noble banister? No one who once leaves the first arrondissement ever makes a return pilgrimage. Its charm is fortuitous, made up of friendly encounter and familiar regard. That grocer's shop, ensconced at Saint-Eustache like a mollusc in its marine rock, sells early vegetables to the court of King Louis XII.

I needed a high, airy, light apartment. All those I mourned shone with only fitful gleams, sparks set against beautiful deep shadows, polished surfaces where log and coal fire danced and cat and carpet shared the same grey-blue of twilight. My friends joined in singing the praises of Neuilly, the sea air of the Butte, the Left Bank with its small gardens. I let them talk and kept silent about my plans until the day when I assembled a few guests round a leaden flan and a bowl of hot wine at the very top of Claridge's.

Two small communicating rooms under the roof, a bath, two small twin balconies beside the gutter, some red geraniums and some strawberry plants in pots, most of my furniture, and all my books on the walls. The building—Claridge's Hotel—was a massive one. In addition, my numbered cabin adjoined the thick party wall so that no one passed my door. A cupboard converted by two electric points into a kitchenette where I could boil pasta, eggs, fruit, water for coffee and milk for chocolate; from below there ascended the *plat garni* of the restaurant and warmth in the pipes; as a bourgeoise devoted to household duties, with a modicum of unconventionality, the errant stay-at-home had taken her precautions. 'And where will you be in a fortnight's time?' guffawed my friends.

They laughed too soon. Four years later we were still enjoying the sun and the fresh air on the same balconies, the cat, the dog and I. How simple things were then. Of course we all played our part, animals and people, from the charming director to myself, not forgetting the Claridge's carpenter who made me a table for writing in bed and refused all payment.

'But look,' I told him, 'I want to pay, if it's only for the wood in the table. . . .'

He hid a young girl's smile behind an enormous moustache.

'Don't take on about the wood. I nicked it, a bit here, a bit there. . . .'

At the summit of this 'palace' I led my silent, unsociable working life. At night, leaning out over the swift river of the Champs-Elysées, with its moving headlights, I could see the night birds going and coming, more rapidly than the cars. For the fauna of Paris changes with the district. In my floral gutter at Claridge's there swam, I assure you, a tree-frog. 'Can I believe my senses?' cried the cat when she saw it, stammering with excitement. On summer nights there might be found those large attacus butterflies that damage themselves buffeting against the street-lamps, or the little hawk-moth on the flower-filled windows.

Only a brief excursion by lift from top to bottom, bottom to top, of the hotel, kept me in contact with varied humanity. Englishwomen descended, arrayed for dinner in sea-green Liberty dresses and pink chiffon. The Indian princes never occupied less than an entire floor, accompanied by their wives, their children, their retinue of servants, their private orchestras; and, for weeks at a time, I was diverted by saris woven in gold and silver, embroidered musicians, the faint sound of plucked strings, a spiced perfume. The fine eyes, the dark and firmly-modelled lips of the Indian children, their gravity and their jewels, dispensed throughout the hotel corridors an atmosphere of silent magic.

A Moroccan pasha who arrived all in white in fine wool and muslin, and bespattered with diamonds, came down the following day unrecognizable in a serge suit and trilby. I came across one once at the bottom of the swimming-pool in the nearby Lido. The candidates for the title of 'Miss Universe' hid themselves under the striped tent erected for them on the pavement of the Champs-Elysées, lunched meagrely, dined resentfully, wiped away make-up and tears. Political banquets blocked the lounge. . . .

But, spared all this on the sixth floor, my two cells flourished, nursing the silence of great height and a surprising peace. Discoveries! Everywhere the unknown, the new, the unobserved, arise in our tracks if we but make a move. The floor-waiter, quite pasty from chronic insomnia, white at knees and elbows, is a living creature; he talks, he has travelled, he observes, he desires

to please and even to love. He knows how to proffer a disinterested rose, a recipe from his own part of the world—he has
a home, a family, a sweetheart. . . . There is warmth everywhere
if we only hold out our hands to it, fan it with our breath. I've
received such gifts, right in the midst of one of those places we
think heartless. The chambermaid on my floor was a slender,
sickly Basque, a frail shadow whose hands had to make up
twenty-two beds every twenty-four hours. Her body stayed bent
over all day from it. In return for a few boxes of phytine that
I gave her, how did she repay me during the time—nine weeks—
that I was afflicted with a ghastly shingles? She went to the
linen-room for good threadbare sheets that she insisted on
changing and ironing every day. . . . Strangers, persons unknown,
how gentle you become when we are sensible enough to beckon
to you!

A writer can work well in a hotel. In his own home he takes
up too much room. People are a nuisance, he's a nuisance. But
the hotel porter lies with gusto to protect 'the lady who writes'.
The world's noises stay below when you take the lift, even a loud
burst of music fails to cling to the climbing cage.

One day, when I was going up to my establishment, a well-
dressed man, grey at the temples, saluted me vaguely out of
politeness. 'Madame doesn't know M. Alexandre?' asked the
lift-man. 'M. Alexandre, the great financier?'

Not long after, the great financier ceased to call himself
Alexandre. From then on he was known as Stavisky,[13] during the
revelation of a scandal, his vain flight, and the badly-managed
suicide far away in the corner of a room. The newspaper photographs showed him fallen crosswise, head against a radiator.

For hotel life still produces its blundering or skilful wild men,
its naïve, conceited bandits. There persisted deep in M. Alexandre
the little oriental given to patent shoes and loud suits. Perhaps he
could wear the Pope's tiara, a fez, the *pschent*, without ridicule,

but he was impossible beneath a Parisian hat. It seems to me that, stripped of his clothes, there would have been little more left of him than of one of those skinny hermit-crabs who roam about in an over-large shell. The denouement of his drama scattered a noxious fallout. But many another palace drama remains unfulfilled, leaves the numbered room to end up far away against the piles of a bridge, to culminate in a dance-hall or a *train de luxe*, to bespatter a staircase with blood. The murdered woman, the lunatic, the two lovers locked in self-sought death—let's see, weren't they that very woman in the pink chiffon dress, the man who apologized to himself for running into a door, that greying couple who seemed so bored? Maybe. But already they disappear. Hotel ghosts are ghosts without tenacity.

It may well be that, if Claridge's Hotel had not failed financially, I should still be living there. Four times four seasons seemed short to me there. Sun and wind came straight at me, bringing into my room the jostled fragrance of the red geraniums that I raised in boxes. Tempted by my airy peace, friends came to pass the time, settled themselves beside the same roof, were bored there, went on their uncertain way. Through the flimsy doors there filtered their individual and recognizable perfumes, the smell of old felt spread by the five o'clock whiskies, the penetrating indiscreet aroma of opium after midnight. . . . I had several kinds of friends there: restless, dissolute, hardworking; all were marvellously careful to remain silent and self-contained, as if their silence was the best response they could offer to the silence of my eyrie.

Moving relatively frequently, have I done more than offer my successive apartments marks of regret and attachment, reiterated proofs of my stay-at-home nature? 'Then why move?' you say.

And why not, if one wants to? For a long time now I've continued to stay in my strongholds twenty hours out of the twenty-four. In that same period, readers, you spend ten hours away from home, to return in ill-humour. When there sounded, at Claridge's, the knell of a break-up that shattered the entire service and cooled the furnaces, I go no further than the truth when I say that I bundled my possessions in a dust-cover and leaped across the avenue of the Champs-Elysées to where the odd side welcomed me in an eighth-floor flat, all vanilla cream and hairpins.

It served me right that I was to savour, as if I'd asked for it, something I'd never encountered before and don't want to encounter again—I mean the lightning decrepitude that strikes certain hurriedly-constructed buildings—and that I was punished for it. I didn't have to wait long for the fruits of my presumption; a draught that blew shut a door on the second floor cracked my wall on the eighth floor from floor to ceiling. After which my next door neighbour dropped in to confide in horrified resignation that the roof-terrace was in process of collapsing into her apartment. Not long after, around three o'clock one night, I woke with a start to step into a good twelve inches of water covering the floor. In the bathroom, which was navigable by now, the cat had taken refuge on a porcelain reef and was clamouring for Noah's Ark. Then the first June storm irrupted, hail-shod, breaking the windows and wrenching the window-sashes from their frames.

With so much evidence—and I haven't told all—I had no doubt that the new apartment was a place to laugh about, though it gave me cause for tears too. But I wasn't so stupid as to take it seriously. I adopted the attitude of enjoying a phase that could not last very long. I loved the ship's ladder, swaying in the wind, that we took to the main terrace, the cat on my shoulder, the bulldog suspended in my grasp by the skin of her

neck. Up above, a magnificent observation-post made up for
everything. We watched the horizon stir and move towards us,
the clouds gesticulate, the majestic curtains of rain advancing on
Paris; the lightning struck a sugar-candy Sacré-Coeur and the
greenish hump of the Opéra . . . and on starry nights the odours
of a Parisian summer—bruised lawns and muddy fountains—
rose slowly up to us.

Twenty yards of rather porous balconies, a terrace of more
or less tarred felting, a clutch of lifts, doors one could dismantle
with the aid of a pocket-knife—what's more, they did take them
down sometimes, at night—the sparingly rationed fuel oil for the
central heating, one shouldn't assume that these fragile realities
did not allow a certain degree of fantasy. Some ticks as large as
hazel-nuts that had arrived, I believe, with a load of firewood,
paraded in all directions; and the bulldog could not prevent a
necklace of ticks from embedding themselves round the margins
of her ears like so many pearls. Until I got rid of them for her
she assumed a wholly unexpected resemblance to Mary Stuart.

Beyond balconies and catwalks, what could be seen of the
Champs-Elysées seemed hardly more real to me than a dream.
No detail gave any sign of permanence or interest. Twenty little
brisk and animated goings-on kept me in good humour up there,
including such grand spectacles as processions, military parades,
national funerals, a thousand-footed crowd-caterpillar, floral
cakes and wreaths. . . . At the first outbreaks of rioting I was
even able to believe that it would end up in fountains of shattered
glass on which a rainbow played fitfully.

One day, having left the quaking building to prospect along
the avenue Montaigne for what was said to be a favourable spot,
I took fright at the reception room with its Renaissance chests
and double doors in imitation leather, the dining-room suitable
for a provincial club, the bathroom as mauve as Edouard
Detaille's[14] *Le Rêve*, and fled, to end up in another, better-baited

trap. This consisted of a real bargain—again!—in the place
Vendôme, in the roof, the mansard floor where the windows look
like clock-faces. Oh, to dream above the jam of taxis, nonchalantly leaning against a clock! Oh, ever-present Napoleon,
with his little skirt and his laurel!

An upsurge of commonsense bore me away at the very moment
that a minor miracle came to meet me halfway and offered me
Gustave Quinson's apartment, the one I had been waiting for
in my 'tunnel'. I need hardly say that I ran all the way.

I like to believe that some enchantment preserves at the Palais
Royal everything that's shaky but endures, that crumbles but
doesn't collapse. During my ten years' absence some 'newcomers'
had moved into the rue de Valois, rue de Montpensier or de
Beaujolais. Those with a genuine aptitude for digging themselves
in soon acquire good manners, exchange a mild neighbourly
'Good-day', abandon open-air dialogues for home visiting. They
know that the leavings—when there are any—are divided among
all the animals jointly, and that the crumbs of the leavings are
for the birds. They conform to our pleasant usages; face to the
sun, back against a warm pillar, a chair in place of a table and
a glass of infusion instead of tea, we know how to make a
drawing-room of the garden, discreetly. You who, like me, have
chosen to live in this beautiful place, adhere to its conventions.

Let me be your guide through this restored domain. If you
live here, you must earn your seniority, the only kind that counts
here. Be the lady who uses a stick, the gentleman who grows little
cacti at his window, the gentleman who makes his morning tour
of the garden in straw sandals. One day, perhaps, a small boy
in the garden will solemnly put one of his marbles in your hand.
Perhaps a venerable and ceremonious lady will pay her respects
to you with an 'Ode to Victor Hugo' of which she is the author.
Take care not to sneer at these silent and somewhat mysterious
contributions. They are the small change of a mutual courtesy

and seal your letters patent as citizen of the Palais Royal, town-
ship within a town, city within the city, that chance has restored
to me complete a second time.

Here comes the woman—still young, a brunette with fair hair
—on professional patrol. She is not the only one. Once she asked
me for a signed copy of one of my books.

'Which one would you like?'

'I'd like the saddest one,' she replied.

Her predecessor, who passed to and fro for ten years, lacked
so much modesty and sociability. The very vigour of her profile
clearly showed that she perpetuated an ancient but dying race.
She was a tall and robust old woman who styled herself a genuine
countess and made no bones about her seventy-one years. In
winter she made long gaiters out of newspaper, tied together with
string. She behaved like a camper, rather than a courtesan; you
could see her in the early morning washing at the pavement
hydrant. And if you showed any surprise she would smile at you
with her magnificent, dark, sapphire-blue eyes.

What has become of the former night-walkers of the arcades,
creatures of the night and at home in it? Where is the tall grey
man whose whitish face seemed covered with strange make-up,
unless it was some pasty illness? He sought the shadow of the
pillars and I never knew what kind of vice or hope he cherished.

From time to time a city such as ours sees its scum vanish, the
foetid pockets of its strata emptied. Suddenly Paris vomits, dissolves the shameful part of her attractions, mingles hardy virtues
with inconstant chastity. The most crowded path in the Palais
Royal leads to Notre-Dame-des-Victoires. This is a church where
all come to slake their thirst, as if at the village fountain. The
oyster-seller turns up the corner of her blue apron and pays a
neighbourly five-minute call at Notre-Dame. The greying
delivery-boy lays down his parcels, lights his candle, crosses
himself and departs. A thin young woman is assiduous, her face

in her hands; it's Gaby Morlay, who comes from a remote quarter to make her novena at the church she prefers.

In the time it takes to walk two hundred steps, to take the short cut past the 'cravat clinic' and one end of the Galerie Vivienne, I plant a small flame on a thorn of the burning bush like everyone else. The church is warm with petitions, candles and gratitude. Between the services there is complete silence, but every stone is engraved, and speaks. How many candles, how many tears!

While I write the swallows susurrate and announce to the garden their recent arrival. They do not think about their departure in the autumn. And I? I'm very far from wishing to depart. Am I not still occupied, somewhere in Paris, with the plumber and his adolescent apprentices, the curled wood shavings that escape the plane, the nails they call *cavaliers*, the hem of the curtain when it is drawn, when it is open, the waltz the painter sings, the 'Where am I?' of first waking? Everything holds me here. But the swallow does not know that it will depart in the autumn. How should I surpass in wisdom the most migratory of birds?

Maiden Voyage of the Normandie*

I wanted to have the *Normandie* all to myself. I can see now that this isn't at all easy, even if one leaves one's bed and cabin at dawn. In these long days the dawn lacks mystery. The deep austere red, the sanguine rending colour of most births, soon changes to gold; and the spindly clouds, motionless at sea-level, are warmed, lighten, and take off.

I wanted at this ambiguous hour to possess the *Normandie* while all on board were asleep; but a ship never sleeps. The cleaning watch, thirty-nine silent men, start work at two in the morning and the ship's interior lights never go out, night or day.

Never mind! At half-past five the smooth black armchairs grouped round the space of the bridge attract only a shadow council, presided over by an enamel paladin, and the great saloon is quite empty.

In the winter garden a strange silence still prevails amongst the birds, who are not, however, all dead. But it's a risky fate for a Bengali on board, so near the bows and subject to the impetuous wind our speed creates.

No one in the blue swimming-pool, no one in the bar. The gymnasium offers ghostly athletes, a vaulting-horse, an inert bicycle, a camel-hump, a rowing machine—all that moves and rocks and bounds but remains motionless, teasing in silence the

55

flexed muscle. All her light ablaze, the *Normandie* offers a fête
to the invisible.

An empty corridor is good to look at when it is so long that
the parallel lines of floor and ceiling seem to converge and join
in the distance. Not a solitary passenger. Now and again the blue
back of one of the men on watch disappears as soon as it is
glimpsed. If I lost my way, could I, by running, catch the man
in blue and ask him? But he must be a dream man and such
men never reply.

Climbing, descending, nothing stops me. The doors obey me
with hallucinatory meekness.

Squirrels, cats and dogs, painted on the walls of a play-room,
have been begging since last night and sleep standing, waiting
for the children to waken them.

Here I am, breathless, under the welcoming low ceiling of the
tourist class. But now I lose my way. I shout 'Hi! You there!'
to a man in blue I glimpse—or his shadow, it must be his shadow
—who stumbles against the half-drawn curtains of the theatre
in front of me and slips between them. I slip in after him but
come out again alone soon enough. It's certainly not for me that
a single star of feeble light shines in the gloom, right over the
middle of the stage. The scent of white lilies that greets the end
of the night turns the stomach a little; and if I were to meet a
man in blue, a real one who was not just a deceptive silhouette, a
reflection gliding along the walls of polished metal, I'd ask him
for the nearest gangway. Still, even if there's not the least trace of
a man in blue, the great cold breeze finds and delivers me.

Gaiety of the still-young morning, hardly explored. Beyond
the decks extending behind us the wide skirt of our wake opens
to mark our passage on the sea. But the *Normandie* is no longer
mine alone; I share her with the men of the cleaning squad, still
silent and furtive. These, real enough and in fours, seem to dance
the ship's toilet meticulously, lovingly, rhythmically. On the lowest

deck, grateful to the bare feet, a prostrate carpenter uses an adze to smooth down an imperceptible bump on the planking. After each light stroke of the adze he feels the place, scratches, looks for the induration like a surgeon; he won't leave until he's sure it's cured.

The morning sun and wind whet the appetite. Anyway, it's time to yield the domain that dawn has lent me to its hosts. In the dining-room, with its translucent walls, a battalion of impeccable stewards have returned to life, if not to motion, under a basilica ceiling and in the glare of a forest of luminous pillars. As far as the eye can see there are icebergs, frosted and giant, crystal organs. I'm alone and almost afraid to order what seems, in contrast, to be the smallest white coffee in the world.

Arrival

We shall never see this again, we shall never forget it. We are still in quarantine but the impatient city has dashed out to meet us. A flock of multicoloured aeroplanes and helicopters surrounds us, toasts us, showers us with paper petals. The sea around us tosses as many small boats as waves. The crowd, storming the bridges, mingle their cries with those of the sirens. Fragments of the Marseillaise throb in the wind, gathered by our hearts in passing, saluted by our hoarse voices, for we all taste the joys of being simple, of feeling young and excited, dazzled and grateful for a welcome surpassing anything we had imagined.

Behind a blue mist rise a group of skyscrapers that slowly grow to pierce the mist with their summits, presenting to the sun facades whose boldness is unequalled by any other human edifice. In two hours we shall be at their feet.

We do not easily submit to the ugliness of an architecture. On the other hand, we are eager to adopt what is beautiful. Beauty is the thing that most quickly ceases to astonish. After the first shock, the first, almost religious, thrill that strikes us dumb before New York seen from its port, we are happily at home with the harmony of its organ tones, its tiers, its giant termitaries pierced by sparkling eyes. An underground city will always excite our apprehension. But what more natural than for man to assault the sky? Throughout time he has scaled mountains, planned towers, coveted wings. His impetuosity is manifest here with an audacity so deliberate and so headstrong as to impose a style and engender an art.

Singular observation : while the skyscrapers, seen from the *Normandie* through the warm mist, remain only blurred peaks, the larger for their vagueness, they resemble a grove of churches, a gothic bouquet, and remind us of that Catholic art that hurled its tapered arrow towards heaven, the steeple stretching up in aspiration.

Half seen, New York is as romantically decked out as the cities that emerge, pennate and spiky, from the dreams of Gustave Doré, Victor Hugo, even Robida. All derived from the cube, faithful to the simple or multiplied quadrilateral; a mysterious law of occasion and proportion nevertheless ensures that the one is beautiful, pleasing eye and spirit, while the other becomes heavy, spoiled by its own height, climbing and contracting by massive gradations.

From the height of my thirtieth floor I overlook only a few of their terraces and landings, where tenants, pigeons and banked vegetation dwell together. But I already want something higher than the highest terraces.

I should like, I think, to live for a time in this small Louis XIII castle, with six windows to its frontage and a slate roof, set on the summit which it crowns like an inkstand on a desk. I should enjoy no less the eyrie of climbing medieval stones, a kind of observatory or giddy houselet, that I can only see by turning my head upside down. But it's not the day to satiate myself with these sights. A stormy twilight of unbroken deep blue settles on this unknown city, over which I should like to see the evening star blossom. But there is no evening star in New York.

The night is suddenly made manifest by fiery serpents, by rectangular constellations, by eclipses and resurgences, red spheres in clusters outlined in blue volcanic phosphorus, heralds of the Last Judgment, celestial pathways blazed with pearls, fountains, droplets, stars and comets; by bonbons showering from a fiery rose, infernal violet and the green of spring. It is not fatigue, or the purgatory of the Customs, or the temptations down below that matter. Nothing is urgent but to remain here, between the perfume of the large, sweet oranges and that of the green lilies, ice-water within reach, leaning out till midnight over the flashing New York night.

Midnight Sun

Copenhagen (July-August)

It is a strange and fleeting comfort to move about in a city too large for its pedestrians or wheeled traffic. Not many on foot, everyone on two wheels. Here, movement becomes detached from human sounds—horns, grinding gears, bells, but no voices. A dreamlike smoothness. No abuse, no conversation, a life that glides and smiles, but does not speak.

At Tivoli there is an open-air theatre in the gardens where a pantomime is performed. A pantomime, naturally. No voices. Music, old and French. The screams from the riders on the switchback provide the pleasure and illusion of a crime committed in the open air. Otherwise, see Luna Park, but a Luna Park in limbo.

The Bourse, topped with a strange, pointed, spiral confection. Seen close-up, it's made of dragons' tails twisted in a Cambodian tendril.

Elsinore. You like it? Neither do I. Let's move on.

Fish, crustaceans of Copenhagen, soft, round, salted, dried, cured, pickled—the water spurts under your tongue when you cut up the flower-bed of shrimps' tails, crimson on a bed of black bread dusted with cumin. Deception: the shrimps have been cooked in fresh water; and the prawns are for pale persons.

Fjords. All that scatter of islands and rocks! Debris of the shore, flung down like coffee-grounds. The coast emerges, becomes rocks and stones, then populous, closes in on the port side, closes in to starboard. A gay row of wooden houses, partly in mourning, white with black outlines, black with white outlines. Every dimension of human life is there on a small scale—little houses, minute gardens, lighthouses at ground level; man is tolerated here so long as he does not stand up. But the red cow wants to be as venturous as the wild goat and plants herself on the rocks. Pure green patches of grass, narrow spotless pastures. The sky and the water receive from each other a bluish milk.

Fjords. Water imprisoned by the shores; intricacies and barriers of reefs; the *Eros* seems to open its own passage, which every moment appears blocked. Small puffing boats, small houses, painted barriers and fences—to confine what?—and flowers on the window-ledges. It's apparent that man's a mere appendage to the landscape here.

Bergen. The lengthening of the day. At ten o'clock it's pink, next day at eleven it's yellow and blue. Midnight, the 17th of July, is twilight. At five in the morning a brave ten o'clock sun is at the zenith. Tonight, at eleven, Léopold Marchand and I play bezique on the bridge and the pink band of sunset does not leave the sky. Boats play around the *Eros* carrying young girls and young men in swimming costumes, gramophones, even a saxophone.

A lad, two lads, undress, dive in quite naked and swim for
half an hour. Records play Navarro's song.

At two in the morning my cabin is inundated with light.

Bergen offers more than it promised. We'd need to make many
trips before we became tired of the fish market, where the fat fish
have polished the stones, the gabled houses, the phallic unicorn,
the wooden lanes whose stench ends in a green garden at the
bottom. Fried eggs are eaten cold. The house of the Hanseatic
League shows one how apprentices were lodged and disciplined
in the sixteenth century: cupboard-beds with doors sliding in
grooves and a bull's pizzle well-polished by use. Codfish to bring
luck have floated against the ceiling, gaping, for two hundred
years.

Brandt and its furs. They're all beautiful. But which one to
covet? Anyway, their prices bridle enthusiasm. Quilts of birds'
feathers? No sachet could dispel the smell of camphor, oil and
ancient death.

Between Bergen and Trondhjem

The tricks of the light begin. Last night, three hours of magic,
improbability, deception. How to describe them? Great rain-
laden masses of clouds disputing the sky, pierced by the sun
towards ten in the evening so that a localized fiery flux spreads
over the sea round a long, massive column composed of real
sunlight, stretching to the ship like a gangway. But the rest of
the sea belongs to the cold colours of flowers and of the moon;
on one side the wake is the bluish colour of moleskin, on the
other as green as the flat scum on marsh-water. The rocky desolation (all those Ararats without an Ark) that accompanies us

climbs and loses all its verdure save for a velvety moss, blackened and fiery. Walls, fortifications, defences against the heavens, a parapet more than a thousand metres long that will never suffer human tread.

Eleven at night : the sun, about to touch the sea, strikes violet rays on the highest rocks. One hillock is the colour of decayed liver, a sudden sparkling green at the base. A purple haze floats between two mountainsides. The world closes in before us, our voyage seems to be ending against shelves, ridges, shoulders, one piled behind the other, themselves overwhelmed by vapours heavy with imminent rain. To our left a possible passage opens, narrow and difficult, along the flank of a great wall a thousand metres high—then the scene changes again. Spits of land gilded green with precious pastures; well-painted farms with their feeble illumination; and the scent of new-mown hay floating to us over the still water. O earth . . . dedication of grass and flowers, irresistible homage. . . .

Beneath the red and pink streak where the sun has died a fine village stretches along one shore. No one sleeps during this eternal day, hands and voices wish us godspeed. . . .

Midnight. The sleeping sun awakes, the herald of the dawn, pale as young barley; day engendering day without the intermediary of night.

Boredom of a country without night. Hunger for obscurity, thirst for its philtres, even for its sicknesses. I love the night, the moonglow, the seasons, the troubled darkness, the blacker than black, the less than black. . . .

Mölde. A pleasant bathing place. A desirable haven for the traveller. Vegetation thick up to the muddy seashore. Hay hanging on its rails—here they dry the hay like washing. Meadow flowers, murmur of trees, a Swiss softness of scene. We climb to the hotel panorama three kilometres away where lunch, served by pink, well got-up young girls, costs a little more than a hundred francs a head, with mild beer and a 'margaux' tasting of liquorice and plums. The daughter of the house, a childish giantess, fixes nasturtiums in the crowns of the folded napkins. Heat—nordic style. It would be too much for a native of Saint-Tropez.

Aalesund. We need fresh water; the water-tanker comes nonchalantly to our aid.

Fjord still. But the most beautiful, especially at twilight between the high banks, innumerable cascades, the snow near. The snow-water gradually disturbs that of the sea-passages, pouring in a milk impossible to paint—luminous, opaque, bright violet in the raw shadow of a rockface, blue in the sun, imprinting its colour on the belly, the spread wing, of the skimming gull. Over this water, which is like any coloured substance save water, we reach at the eleven o'clock twilight the spatulate *cul-de-sac* where Mérok lies.

Mérok. A few houses, five or six inevitable traders selling post-cards, bracelets, brooches, local costumes, carved wooden toys and the famous knives. But the cascade, which falls from the skies, is opulent—a watery powder, a frostfall of battered water, a foaming impetuosity. All the rest, a circle of rocky peaks, completely shut in save for our approach corridor, is a prison. And the water smells dully of the lake; the mud is beneath—the mud that, at certain times, extends in banks and keeps off the fish. We

Colette's birthplace at St Sauveur en Puisaye

Colette in 1928

have cast anchor in a watercolour of opalescent milk; from above, next day, we look down at the shore, the slime that is the mud. Arriving, cries of 'How marvellous! We must stay five or six days at least! The walks, the mountain picnics, the long footraces, the. . . .'

Next day: 'How bloody boring it is here! The eye is bruised by everything. The open sea, quickly!' And we depart surreptitiously in the morning, having satisfied our pioneering conscience by an otherwise admirable excursion, an hour by car and fifteen hundred metres into clear air, up to the soiled and fissured summer snow, up to the lake in the heights, up to the hotel by the lake and the fake 'Lapp encampment' selling woollen gloves and postcards. But the little reindeer is very charming, with the young velvet on its antlers and its long virginal eyelashes. Photos, photos. The flowering reed, a plume of spun glass, abounds; and, lower down, the wild strawberry, the blackcurrant, and the large-fruited redcurrant.

Seville: Holy Days

A bush bristling with lights advances, carried by performing penitents. Other penitents, exhausted, rest on one leg. The tram moves at the pace of the procession, and so does the music provided by the tobacco factory nearby.

The cathedral is unbearable. Vertical forests of sculpture and red velvet. Maybe there is something magnificent up there beneath those vaults—but they are farther off than the heavens —something that takes its ease in the air and will not come down to us, like a vulture. Hateful priests—two, ten, a hundred—who talk loudly and pace the flags with thicksoled step; it's obvious that God is their private carpet.

More combs and mantillas than I'd hoped for—it's Holy Week—a fashion invented to heighten the woman who is short, round, low-buttocked.

At the café concert at night. A worn-out Spanish dancer dances. A long yellow muslin dress to hide the years sweeps the floor with a sound of scuffed shoes. All her life she's worn the old corset, which squeezes her stomach, compresses her waist under the breasts, and makes the pelvis seem wide and long in contrast. She is pre-Toulouse-Lautrec.

The star, Rosa Casa, dances well. But she appears at the end

66

in a little tunic in which she feels naked, so keeps her elbows to her sides and her knees close together. She is the prisoner of her skin and dances what she calls the 'charleston' as paralysed as a bourgeoise.

Toledo, we must not forget Toledo, my word no! And, in Toledo, the El Greco museum. But nothing can make me like El Grecos. Especially the El Grecos in the museum! The slanting noses of all the El Grecos, those noses of chalky bone, the downy marabouts' beards of the El Grecos. Ugh, I knew it!

And then there's Charles II! Just think of Charles II. Fortunately he's close by. Mouth like a sick cherry, his angel's hair combed on top—the lice stayed beneath—his azure armour and ravishing pink sash. A good job that's over, I can look at the streets, the deep, narrow scene, and people's faces and the round plaza: 'Real Marzipan' on one side, 'Toledo Marzipan' on the other. Between the two one can drink good beer. But . . . where is the lavatory? The patron, at the zinc counter, asked very quietly, straightens up and calls loudly to his son: 'Pepe! Show the señora to the lavatory!' He points to the stairs. Pepe hurries forward. But first he has to shout piercingly to his older sister: 'Maria! Where's the key?' The sister bustles up, takes down a key from the shadow, pushes aside a group of standing drinkers to give it to her brother. 'This way, señora!' I mount, followed by twenty looks, and much speculation. . . . The stairway is full of soldiers. They stand aside courteously at the child's injunction 'Let the señora pass!', form in line, and wait till I've opened and then closed behind me a door where the Toledan child will watch faithfully outside. . . .

Andalusia.—It's fine good land, well looked after. The spring is well advanced, which makes everyone gay. They seem to be gay because of not being in Castile. They're well off. April comes to greet us, then it's May, soon June. The green shoot of the barley, then the unfurled leaf, at last the flower.

Trujillo.—A vaulted inn, white, a convent for eating in. Our taxi-driver—hailed in Madrid in front of the Hotel Alfonso XIII —thinks we can stay the night here. Why not? The girls are pretty, followed and coveted by men in pointed hats, the goats are dipped in henna, the sheep well-fleeced, white with chestnut heads. And there's a little wood! I've been crying for a wood ever since Madrid!

The coast—pink earth, umbrella pines, almost like Provence. The European Rif, stifling in the twilight, turns violet, dense, complex, then melts into night, from which emerge obscure humps and peaks on which vertigo balances. Algeciras? It's nothing. But a sad nothing. The Casino is a blackish tooth. Its balcony has been shaped by the sea's bad humour. An English oasis, the garden and hotel are anglicized and floral and occupied by English people—we don't bother them, they just ignore us. A miserable old tub to cross the Hespérides. A little ancient thing in which ten French (ourselves included) wonder if it's necessary to be seasick. We arrive before the decision and the Hespérides leave us sinking between two solid waves in a small contraption of a boat, wet all over, that wallows rather like a sunfish.

Rome in Winter

Christmas 1917

The closeness of a greenhouse where a spray of water has just moistened the foliage, a sun of bright silver, at every step the scent of carnations and mimosa, of peeled oranges, bunches of celery, apples, violets—what May month has so much perfume, so much of spring, as this Christmas morning in Rome?

Yesterday the train pushed cautiously through blankets of snow near Modane. The day before, Paris, without lights, shivered under the rain. Today the Capitol gardens, sprinkled with birds, glisten with a greenery barely tarnished by winter.

This day, the entire week, belongs to the children. A carpet, a moving layer, covers the steep stairway that climbs to the church of Santa-Maria in Aracoeli. A hundred steps of children, Italian children brown as ants, with the sound of cicadas—a thousand children, clinging to this stony hillside like their fathers to the flanks of the Carso, shriek, chatter, buy and sell. These sharp little temple merchants deal in bonbons, toys, statuettes, holy images—especially the portrait of the Bambino of Aracoeli, set in gilt and cut gem-stones.

It takes a good deal of perseverance to reach the church through the shouts, the beguiling offers, the bold entreaties and the lisped imprecations. What's more, the impudence of these

69

Roman brats is in no way tempered under a ceiling whose lavish gilt ages too slowly. They scream and struggle in front of the monumental crib where, as well as the three royal Magi, a peasant woman carries gifts : white cheeses, oranges and figs, Italy's tribute, roll at the feet of the gold-banded Bambino. In order to see the Bambino, and the pasteboard angel and the grey ass, the urchins jostle each other, give each other a leg up one of the smooth pagan columns, and clusters of children garland the edges of a font like a decorative pattern.

To the right of the entrance a pulpit trembles under a weight of child-preachers. Sermonizers four to eight years old, prophetesses barely out of nappies and nursery school; every child may preach during Christmas week. One inspired girl— seven years old, with a straight nose, hair like Medusa's serpents and tragic eyebrows—contests the field of eloquence with a four-year-old tribune who is full of deliberation and wisdom but intimidated by the crowd. Victorious, the little girl bows to the audience and speaks—declaims, I should say—calls Heaven to witness, evokes *i soldati*, appeals to the Gesù Bambino. I can't see any difference between this pathetic child, stamping her foot on the platform and extending her fist towards the gilt ceiling, and the young star of the Italian cinema that she will become in ten years' time : the same over-expression, the same instinct for the generous gesture, the same lack of moderation, nuance and personality.

Behind the pulpit is a group quarrelling in low voices, a handful of women whose fine hair is half covered by folded handkerchiefs—heavy mothers, superb but rather bulky adolescents. Each flaunts her own infant prodigy, pushes it forward into the pulpit, and whispers the forgotten phrase. There are envious glances, dark menaces, mocking laughter; in fact, despite the Pinturicchio frescoes close by, this jealous corner smacks less of a church than of the wings of a theatre.

31st December

Half-past eleven. Dinner, the last dinner of the year, was, for Frenchmen, so cordial, so full of hope, so friendly, that we forgot all about Rome. The night—a pale blue, grey almost, quivering with stars—brings us back to Italy. We linger before going in, detained by the calm night, the pale moon, the white electric light. Half-past eleven . . . soon the year will be over. Some lights in the Queen Mother's palace; fifty paces below the monks' kitchen-garden, an extension of the royal gardens, wafts a rural odour of green cabbages and fennel. On the pavement of the via Veneto an open-air florist ties up her last dozen red carnations for a dreaming young soldier. The beggars who were plucking their mandolins beneath the windows have departed. The Christmas tree in the hall of the hotel still bears, in place of its extinct candles, bits of tinsel, a gilded paper star, a globe of blown glass. . . . All that's left is to return to a room, unknown yesterday and forgotten tomorrow, to listen from the balcony's height to the sounding of a hundred midnights from the clocks of Rome.

A first bell chimes, a far-off bell of old cracked bronze; it is answered by a gunshot. Then a whole burst of artillery sounds off. Guns, rifles, heavy shells; a volley that makes one search the sky, in vain, for the glow of rockets, fiery showers, bengal lights —but not a gleam. A sombre celebration, these wartime fireworks that permit only the sounds of war. . . . All the same, the bells and the rifles make a fine victory racket for a moment, the heart swells. . . . Having chimed and thundered midnight, Rome is silent, leaving its fountains to murmur and its unmoving palms to breathe under a sky pale as an African sky.

To look out over this incomparable city, to watch at midnight on the 31st of December, shoulders barely covered—this is, we repeat to ourselves, a surprise, a New Year. . . . Let us repeat

it to ourselves and out loud, say it often enough to prevent
nostalgia for a corner of France slipping in between two con-
gratulatory sighs—that corner where the oil-lamp casts an evening
glow through a solitary window, between the branches of stern
oaks and silver-trunked chestnuts—a corner of France tormented
by winter, yes, agonized by war, muddy, forsaken by its farm
labourers at the front, but for all that beyond compare, cherished
above all else.

Algeria

Desert Flower

We had noticed her on arriving at Bou-Saâda, at the moment when the sunset colours the nearest mountains an unexpected violet and the most distant a pink, pale as red-hot iron in daylight. Fatigue, wonder, three hundred kilometres of desert passing before our novice gaze, the sirocco, the iridescent distance behind a suspended curtain of sand—all these left us dazed and credulous. The same exclamation came from our dust-contaminated lips to greet the brief twilight and the pink reflection borrowed by an almost night sky from sand pinker and more luminous; the rocket-showers of oleanders in flower, the vivid green of palm-groves and palm trees cool on the eye like breaking fountains—the clumsy, powerful flight of a great vulture, a thread of spring water issuing from a burnt mountainside, the aqueous sparkle of a grasshopper's gauze wings with the spread of a swallow.

The little girl we'd noticed was sitting against a crumbling wall of unbaked clay, a few foundering and half-collapsed handmade blocks, all that remained of a native dwelling after a short rainy period and a long drought. She was, perhaps, five years old and pitiful in resplendent finery. Her slim ankles, crossed, bore loose anklets of crude silver; twists of metal chinked on her arms; with barbarian curiosity we touched her tiny feet encrusted with river mud and the delicate, unwashed, henna-tinted hands. She had enormous eyebrows drawn vividly in black across her forehead, a proud tooth-filled mouth with fleshy angles, and languorous, ageless eyes between lids heavy with make-up. A reddish rag was twisted round her hair and two tiny dusty tresses hung in ram's-horn curves over her ears; elsewhere tatters of cotton revealed a slender knee, the hollow flank of a young greyhound. The crumbling wall was exactly the colour of her skin, a pale yellow subtly tinged with pink; and the still child seemed to have been born but a moment before, freshly modelled in light clay, shaped from a handful of desert.

She held out a hand and begged shrilly, in Arabic. We had no change, but Daurces managed to find an unpierced twenty-five centime coin which the henna-tinted fingers grasped.

'*Saha! Saha!*'

With this expression of thanks the little girl jumped up and ran off, raising two wings of sunlit dust at her heels. She looked back once to wave a grateful hand with imperious grace.

Next day we were waiting for a meal in the gardens of the Petit-Sahara, dishevelled and exhausted after the obligatory excursions to the miserable mosque, the stinking, flowered brook where the men washed their linen upstream, the women below the men, the Jews below the women; to the makers of high boots, whose wool-lined legs gripped our calves; to Ben Grada (seller of carpets, bracelets, bulls' pizzles sheathed in orange leather), who gives us flowers, perfumed cigarettes and coffee in porcelain cups; to Zorah, who dances naked but clings to her head-veils and jewellery. . . .

A small brown hand slipped between the railings and held out to us an unpierced twenty-five centime coin. A child's voice babbled throatily in Arabic, the eyes and teeth of the little girl who had said '*Saha! Saha!*' sparkled from beyond the enclosure. . . .

'Oh! it's that charming little creature again! What do you want? Ahmed, what does she want?'

'She's giving you the coin back,' said Ahmed, our burnoused guide. 'She wants local money.'

'Fair enough,' said Daurces.

He took back the coin and gave the desert flower a fine Algerian piece as large as a marigold, embossed with the two palm-trees, a new coin worth two sous, the very thing to dazzle an uncivilized child.

But the small coloured fingers did not close on the coin and 'Saha, Saha' she cooed again. . . .

'How pretty it is, that hoarse wood-pigeon's song! No, Ahmed, don't chase her away, let her be so that we can listen. . . . What's she saying? Is she thanking us?'

'She is saying,' explained Ahmed placidly, 'that you still owe her three sous.'

Ahmed

'Ahmed, you won't forget to come at nine this evening?'

'No, sah.'

'And you'll take us to see Fatma?'

'Yessah.'

'Fatma, or maybe it's Zorah or Yamina or Aïcha . . . you know who I mean? A girl who danced for me last year, a really marvellous girl with bulges just here . . . and there. . . .'

Ahmed interrupts our friend with a gesture and discreetly lowers pale coffee-coloured eyelids over eyes as dark as black coffee. He is still a novice in intrigue. His great eyes are expressionless, but his fifteen-year-old mouth has learnt the European tricks of registering cunning, disdain or mockery, and smiles too often. It's not his fault. He lies in wait for tourists, guides them, listens to the coarse pleasantries of suburbanites who treat themselves nowadays to a three-day trip in place of their former afternoon's boating on the Marne. He is brought in contact with our faults and stupidities. He would imitate them if his thin adolescent body were not constrained to dignity by the burnous.

'You can go, Ahmed.'

He leaves or, rather, he appears to leave. A fold of the pink sand envelops his burnous which, in the desert, assumes a turtledove hue. We are free to go without him, to drink *anis* by the market place, to buy postcards without him under a kind of open shed where they sell fancy liqueurs, cans of petrol and tobacco. Without him we can watch the flocks of sheep passing on their way to the stalls and pity the exhausted ewes dragging themselves along the road. We do not need him to climb to the highest terrace of baked clay above the humble, dark little mosque; once there, we need no guide to show us how to scatter silver and nickel coins on a square of the checker-board of terraces spread beneath us, coins whose tinkling brings running out some naked child, some unveiled young girl who turns a blue-starred cheek to our gaze.

We do not need Ahmed, but he is everywhere with us. Hidden in the brief shadow of a wall dissolving under recent rains. Visible among the stiff, stocky palm trees fed from an underground source, languidly leaning against the railings of the garden surrounding the hotel, Ahmed anxiously observes the infidel Franks until the evening arrives.

He reappears, officially, at the hour when the uneven, tireless beating of drums behind closed doors sound like an anxious heart. He leans on the long staff he uses to chase off the begging children—'*Soldi, Soldi, mistah Amelican*'—and to sound rudely on the doors of the Ouled-Naïl dwellings. He strides ahead of us in the moonless night, lit by the sand like snow, where we hear only the muffled drums, a piercing flute-note falling, rising, falling again, climbing in a minor key with the useless, exhausting obstinacy of a fountain, while the near-cold wind from the mountains rustles the palms and disturbs the sand. . . .

A door opens, a door that Ahmed has struck imperatively. It is that of a slender, preoccupied Zorah, whose deep hue and narrow waist encircled with silver are like those of an ant.

'That's not the one I'm looking for,' says our friend. 'I told you, Ahmed, she's a superb creature, taller than the others, who was called . . . who was called. . . .'

Ahmed is too zealous to wait for the end of the sentence.

'Come, sah, come . . . don't take any notice of Zorah, come. . . .'

The flowing burnous, the long staff precede us to another threshold, another dwelling furnished with a bench, a rattan armchair, a copper bedstead and a rug nailed to the wall. An enormous matron with great leonine eyes and her daughter, a small beauty of fourteen or fifteen, will dance for us if we wish or serve us with tea perfumed with mint. . . .

'No,' says our friend drily. 'Didn't you understand, Ahmed? I want to see that girl again who had plaits like ships' cables and clusters of jewellery in her ears. I remember now, she was called "The Pearl". . . .'

'Yes! Come along, sah, come. . . .'

But he takes us to a charming creature, faded and delicate, with the proud bearing, the dry, princely hand, the dash and aristocracy of the tuberculous. . . .

'You're making fun of me, Ahmed,' says our friend as we leave. 'When I see someone's making fun of me, I don't pay. You won't get a sou for tonight.'

An exaggerated sob troubles the darkness.

'I don't like being taken for a fool,' our hard-hearted friend continues. 'If you'd only told me you didn't know this . . . this Fatma, Aïcha, this Pearl, then. . . .'

Sincerely moved, Ahmed comes close to our friend in the strip of chalky light thrown by an acetylene lamp before the threshold of the last Ouled-Naïl.

'Sah, I know her. But I can't take you. . . . She's . . . she's in bed.'

'In bed?'

'Yessah, ill.'

He sighs, shows the whites of his eyes and adds, theatrically : 'Very ill!'

Our friend studies the young Arab's face suspiciously; it is green in the cruel glare of the acetylene burner.

'Ill? You're lying. What does it matter, anyway, you've lied to me before. Not a sou, d'you hear? Not a sou!'

He turns on his heel but Ahmed clings to him.

'I'll tell you the truth. She's not ill!'

'I don't care. Go away.'

'She's not ill, she's . . . she's gone away!'

'Will you leave me alone?'

'Listen, sah, listen . . . she's gone away, sah . . . listen. . . .'

His protestations follow us as far as the hotel gates, where we find him next morning, humble but tenacious, still hoping for his tip. Our friend, who has learned of the fate of his Pearl this morning, calls him :

'Ahmed! Here, take this, you little scoundrel.'

'Thank you, sah.'

'Didn't you know "The Pearl" was dead?'

'Yessah.'

'Then why did you tell me all that nonsense instead of just saying that she was dead?'

Insensibly, Ahmed detaches the skirt of his burnous from the Roumi's grip. A mysterious and enigmatic pride restores to his still childlike countenance its original dignity, shattered by the grimaces of servility and lying. He turns his head away and answers laconically :

'Not nice. . . .'

Ouled-Naïl

The guide halted before a barely visible door and struck it with his staff. No one came and we could hear only the faint sounds of a party in a distant house—the febrile beating of the large, flat drum, the shrill clarinet shaped like a convolvulus with a long calyx whose piercing sound excites nervous shivers in the skin, and a high-pitched ou-lou-lou-lou. We could hear also a rustling of nearby palms and the pattering of sand carried by the night wind, shifting and raining finely against the walls. Our feet were bathed in a cold white ash moving like a wave that spread a pale luminosity; and this sand and wind, with the cool of the night, made us forget the desert and think of the sea and a small French *plage*.

The burnoused guide banged louder, using the tip of his staff, and a ray of light shone through the cautiously opening door. A clash of bracelets, ear-rings and necklaces came towards us; the reflection from the sand showed us the gleam of eyes and teeth and of pendant jewels dangling round a face. Our guide exchanged a few Arabic sentences with the indistinctly-seen woman. She was obviously protesting vigorously and he brusquely insisting. At last she moved back and invited us to enter.

The glow of a small fire lit on a breast-high hearth shone on her redly; the flare of an acetylene lamp hung on the wall threw brutal, blue-white patches of light here and there on her dark skin.

'This is Yamina,' announced the Arab guide.

Yamina laughed and ceremoniously gave each of us a hand
sheathed in a concentric design drawn with henna. To each of
us she said 'Bonsoar', pronouncing the word like the English
actresses who play in French pieces. Her white cotton skirt, very
wide with a high flounce edged in pink, the square-cut bodice
braided in rose, clothed her in the style of a young girl of 1899.
But her incomparable cigar-coloured feet were bare, save for
silver anklets embossed with little mobile rosettes that jingled
musically; and a belt of silver plaques compressed her waist as
a ruthless fashion demanded.

While she was preparing the green tea we studied her with
our offensive barbarian curiosity. A pink scarf spangled with gold
broadened the outline of her small head. Two great black tresses
followed the contour of her blue-starred cheeks, hidden by a
shower of small chains dangling from her ear-lobes, while bracelets bristling with spikes protected Yamina's delicate arms from
wrist to elbow.

She retained scarcely any oriental modesty, but flirtatiously
poured our cloudy perfumed tea into narrow blue glass goblets
with the brazen cordiality of a bourgeois innkeeper. Seeing her
there, busy poking the bright fire, replacing the kettle on the
embers, offering us sugar, rather suggested some decked-out
housewife, her land with its animals and vineyard outside the
door . . . but outside the door the edge of the oasis was only
twenty yards away, an abrupt boundary to this fertile green
patch lost in the desert. . . .

We were surprised that, despite her blue tattooing, heavy
southern jewellery and made-up eyelids, Yamina glowed with
an almost western beauty, more regular than expressive. . . .

Her easy laugh displayed fine wide teeth, gums purplish-violet
like the flesh of a blood-orange. She could understand, but not
speak, French. Our tea consumed and cigarettes lit, she arranged

us seated along the wall, next to her fine copper bedstead covered with an American eiderdown, called in the drummer and the clarinettist from outside, and danced for us.

Like all the Ouled-Naïl she danced using her arms and hands; her charming restless feet merely brushed the floor as if on hot paving. She danced also using her flanks and the muscles of her energetic little belly. Then she stopped for a moment's rest, using the interval to undo the rose-bordered bodice, the wide-panelled skirt and the chemise of ordinary calico, for the guide insisted that she dance naked. Naked, she returned to the middle of the room between us and the two musicians, who had now turned their backs. The red of the fire and the sinister white of the acetylene flame disputed Yamina's youthful beauty, the slender beauty of a huntress, barely encumbered with breast or rump.

She danced the same dances, knowing no others. But, because of her nudity, she no longer smiled but turned her gaze away from us and refused any longer to meet our eyes. She looked away and above our heads, full of a sovereign gravity and disdain, to seek the distant, invisible desert.

Morocco

Marrakesh

Dazzle of stars and orange-trees. Throbbing of nightingales, twinkling of starlight. The perfume of the orange smothers everything. The grape-fruit in flower has a lingering sweetness that the orange lacks.

The twittering of birds before dawn, a great rushing of birds. After daybreak a cadence of the nightingale echoes still, a fragment of the night. At first light the swallow utters her piercing cry. Then the liquid throaty gurgling of the common oriole and the blackbird. The last songs rise from a damp shingle whose every pebble is the sound of a sparrow and the kisses, kisses, kisses of myriad tomtits. . . .

At noon all fall silent except the dove, always invisible, who murmurs tirelessly through the heat.

The bare wall, flat garden, low firm divan. Surfaces where the eye can wander, the body twist and turn. The irritation of a crease, disgust with a climbing lane. Close by, near the sleeping fountain, an unpleasantly raucous American laugh ruffles the blackbirds' plumage. What's more, this American woman is wearing a chiffon dress printed with a map of Paris. Fact.

Illusion of having reached a goal because one is resting in the middle of an enclosed garden, with only mute signs of human penetration, traces that leave no sound on the air. How long can the illusion last? 'I've come to the very end. . . .' The end of what? Life? Desire? Movement? Love? How long can one browse in the contemplation of a secret garden, a filigree of fine metalwork against a leafy background? How much time can one spend in waiting for the wind at last to stir the rigid, immense torch of a cypress that seems to buttress an angle of the house and create the illusion that the palace itself is swaying?

For today, and the two previous days, the illusion has lasted. It is simply that luxury beguiles one's sense of everyday life; and here, as elsewhere, luxury is stillness and silence.

Who can say what a palace is like before going inside? It is a wall like every other wall, the colour of pale twilight, the colour of earth, the colour of the sky. The men who sit under the portals resemble all the men of these parts beneath every ·Moroccan portal.

At the end of the unpaved passage the small rectangular cloister is so plain and cool and deserted. A chanting of prayers betrays a tiny little mosque, built by the Pasha and reserved for him and his immediate neighbours. No guards or servants to be seen, only the outline of a man dreaming against a door. . . . It puts out an arm to the door, which opens. Again a narrow passage with the beginning of a mosaic surface. At the end of the passage a tall man, all in white, El Hadj Thami Glaou.

The large sunken almost fearful eyes of a dreamer. The small capricious chin of unrestrained violence. We can learn nothing of such a man, save for his studied gentleness, his perfect—almost

wordless—politeness; for he knows nothing of the French
language and stands on ceremony because of this lack, like a
cat who will not drink while watched. He understands everything, or nearly everything. He says little; Samuel ben Rimoj
translates.

He leads us through the long cool rooms, furnished with divans
and scented by burning cedar and coumarin wood.

His own room is a long narrow rectangle, perfume-filled and
flanked by divans with white silk cushions and seats. A bed, all
veiled in white gauze and embroidered in soft pink—the bed of
Clara d'Ellébeuse—is where the ruler of thousands sleeps. His
hand, dark against the white gauze curtain, indicates the
couch. . . .

Dinner in the oriental style, under garish electric light, Dufayel
chandeliers, beside a telephone fixed to the mosaic.

The real luxury—all there is to be seen, perhaps—is the slaves.
Seven or eight women busy themselves round our dining-table of
five places. Beautiful tall negresses, glossier than any fruit, and
dressed in immaculate fabrics, they manoeuvre in their great
skirts like ships on a calm sea. But the fascinating Chleuhs, the
colour of barely-tinted ivory, have fine compressed mouths,
narrow noses and small aristocratic hands and feet. Nothing of
Africa in them. Is there any creature more European than a
young Chleuh dancer, with her Spanish nose and delicate lip?

After the meal she dances while plucking at a small stringed
instrument and another Chleuh sings, stroking a similar instrument with a bow. A third Chleuh sings also; this one is darker,
as attractive as a beautiful Italian girl. Their song is a 'mountain
entertainment', not unlike one from the Tyrol. . . .

Three flights of mosaic stairs. I am supported, carried along,
by two pairs of female arms.

But the two gay recluses are not used to climbing or hurrying;
afterwards they rest a hand on a heaving, plump breast. One is

already done for, enormous with pendulous cheeks; the other is still charming, with small teeth, a frank childlike gaze, expressive little hands with carefully-tended bright red nails. One can only guess at the body beneath the abundant heavy fabrics, fashioned like the dresses of the Second Empire. Cut blue velvet reveals a second robe of heavy rose, floral and magnificent. Over the shoulders straps of violet silk, interwoven with long lozenges of gold, support sleeves of silk brocade. Moroccan head-dress, with silken fringes displaying the ears, a golden plaque above the forehead. This forehead plaque is embossed with fine diamonds; the pear-shaped brilliants dangling from the ears are very European.

The long salon is hung with deeply-reflecting silky Lyons velvet. Standing around us or bent over their mint tea, splendid —almost gigantic—negresses laugh silently.

The Mute

'I am getting divorced,' says the mute.

'Why?'

'Because my wife has run away with another man.'

Planting an index finger in the hollow of a closed fist, he indicates what his wife has left him to do. It is a language universally understood.

In his role of mute he is devilishly cunning. He wants to accompany us to Paris. We have eaten mutton and chicken in the manner of the Glaoui. Also beans with lemon-rind, chicken with an omelette on top, white butter and brown honey, and the half-cooked cake-bread.

We are sprinkled with rose water on the arms, the head, the entire body under the chemise. The caïds of the district, summoned by telephone, have come to greet us on the threshold of the mansion.

Everything is new, the barely-set plaster full of openings, the mosaics, the badly dried ceiling paintings and the empty rooms. The cedar-wood doors perfume the breeze from the nearby mountains. Water floods the heaps of soaked barley. The caïd proudly displays orange-trees, planted two years ago, already bearing fruit. A chilly wind from the heights descends to the hot plain and rushes across with great wings.

The fine peasant figure of the agricultural director, dark and slender. He knows how to laugh—but what a scoundrel he must be! I would prefer being his associate to the risk of being his client.

Gentle slave presence—bare feet, cast-down eyes, friendly hands. A robed child leans against the door-frame, stirring only to move the straw fans that chase the flies away. Oh, the fire of geraniums, the oranges in the young orange-grove!

A market for asses and camels. Noon, a pale sky; everything that exists under this colourless vault is the same forlorn rose colour—the earth, the ramparts, the sobbing camel, the silent ass, the dust-powdered burnous, the bare legs and feet.

Not much sun, but a vertical light soaking through the eyes; the mouth has no saliva, one would like to be quit of one's skin. It is as stupid to defy this time of day as to remain clinging to the bulwarks in a storm. But a Parisienne, like Madame C., defies heat-stroke under a pale pink hat. She has come to the market to buy dishes of plaited straw, 'marvellous for serving fruit in the country, my dear.'

The souk of the dyers. The men, standing upright in vats and coloured rivulets, dripping with vegetable blood, are lacquered a deep violet and there is a greenish gleam on their skin, as yellow as a gourd reflecting thick foliage.

A small square with great fountains where women draw water,

asses drink, the men squat to wash their genitals and backsides before prayers, sprinkling themselves with water from a hand dipped in a bucket.

Souks where skins, made into cushions, handbags or briefcases, spill from little cabins. Copper and brasses roll, cotton goods and hanks of wool are trampled underfoot; but where are the jewels? I want some gold bracelets, so we go to the souk for jewellery.

But do they really sell jewellery there? I see only an uncarpeted floor, three rough wooden partitions, all very squalid. A blond Jew, seated on a plank, leans an elbow on a gimcrack chest. Nothing gleams or catches the eye, there are no smiles for the passer-by. One of the drawers of the chest is opened with difficulty, as if the blond Jew's elbow had closed it for ever. A slender hand gropes within for a gold circlet, a pair of gold bracelets, and an ancient balance folded away in its box like a praying mantis. The stamped-out lamellae weigh in fractions of a gramme. And since I cannot make up my mind, everything goes back into the rough drawer and the blond Jew's elbow seals the chest once more. For these treasures live hidden.

Rabat

Rabat. A small Moorish café above the saltpan. The whiteness of Salé, opposite, becomes blue in the twilight. It's a pity they light so many lamps in the little café. The brilliant red of the geraniums in the garden of the Oudayas fades with the light. Next morning it is cool, even cold, Breton weather. Only the middle of the night recalls the Orient. Round the fountain frogs croak, the stork croaks like a board of dry wood. Thirty francs worth of wood heaped up on a roof serve to make a stork's nest. Female and male are rivals in caution and boldness. Throw in two louis for wash-leather gloves, handkerchiefs and even silks

rifled from balconies. But how beautiful they are, flying or filch-
ing, their wings strung on the arrow whose head is their beak,
its feathers their feet.

Lyautey*

The Residence is gaping and empty but the spring and the
floral decorations dismiss the idea of death. Blue convolvulus
cascading over a foundation of pink pelargoniums hide the building. The heavy braided tassels of the castor-oil plant stitch
together a curtain of yellow jasmine.

Rabat, framed in the great plate-glass window, is the only
object of art in the vast deserted ground-floor room.

A town is always beautiful seen in a rounded or rectangular
setting and, in any event, Rabat-Salé, with their splendid bays
separated by an arm of the sea, are beautiful.

Here a man founded his empire. Is this to be counted against
him? He did not sin through greed. Miraculously, monstrously,
he loved display. At a time when integrity connotes scruffiness he
dared to cherish luxury, conceive palaces, call for gardens and
colonnades, porches, colour, music, roses and carpets. Amongst
those who grudge him this I count the poor in spirit, the long file
of those without underpants, the very same who imposed sump-
tuary taxes during the war without ever having seen a woman's
drawers that were not made of flannel or hemmed cotton.

Bustling with life and activity under Lyautey, the Residence
now slumbers. It waits for Steeg; but what will Steeg bring with
him? Can he adequately fill this new Residence, gleaming with
marble and mosaics, gurgling with streams?

And the one at Fez, where the Marshal's tame birds still sing
in wicker cages hung from arches of roses? Does a dwelling yield
so quickly to one who did not create it, is a garden as docile as

a slave? A woman has departed from this feminine garden, full of roses, sparkling with fountains. She carries it away in her heart, she does not wholly leave it here; a shadow of the garden goes with her and the garden retains a wandering shadow of the woman.

Dinner with the Sultan's chamberlain. Mosaics and lights splash the walls. Beautiful because so vast, the house remains exposed to the moon, which floods in through the top of the open court-yard where water murmurs. The Arab dinner begins with a peppery soup; there follow:

Flaky pastilla with eggs, and sugared chicken
Pigeons
Chicken with fresh almonds
Méchoui
Shad
Mutton covered with olives and lemon-rind
Artichoke hearts laid on well-cooked meat
Mutton served with cooked green apples
Couscous with grapes and chick-peas, served with curds
The Cadi's turban
The Cadi's ears
Orangeade without water
Coffee, mint tea
And, later, milk of almonds.

Fez

We entered the city just when it was readmitting all it had expelled that morning. I made my way into Fez in company with long shadows and orange light, with black sheep and pink

sheep, with donkeys always hoping—but never quite managing
—to sink under their burdens, with idle citizens who had gone
to seek the coolness of the old green river-bed or the ranged slabs
of the ancient cemetery and now returned hand-in-hand. I passed
through the Bab-el-Guissa gate with the punctual black bull,
every day hoping to lead his cows but always following them, a
last poppy in his teeth, complaining loudly and endlessly of
having to leave his fat Moroccan pastures for the dark, stifling
stench of a hidden, perhaps underground, stable just when the
wind begins to stir in the green barley. Alongside me advance,
like a bouquet arranged for St John's Day, ears of milky grain,
rank oats and wild corollas, burdens of flowers and herbage with
the women who gathered them staggering along beneath.

One of these sheaves, walking on two bare horny feet the
colour of the road, came from a field lit with poppies; the other
was blue, not so much from blue flowers as from the flat blue
plaits of young corn.

A camel also crossed the threshold, thin as only a Moroccan
camel can be, its skin dangling in parallel creases over its long
muscles, its large eyelashes powdered with pink dust, the spoil of
a meadow flowery with convolvulus and marigold dangling in
vast panniers. In the furrow traced by its flat feet a file of dried-
up little dappled horses passed, laden with dwarf palms. Here-
abouts the dwarf palm pierces the ground with its tattered fans,
as far as eye can see, good enough fuel for the kilns where they
fire the lime, unless the short hemp of the palm fibre is teased
for weaving.

Sefrou

Paradise on earth, rather as we picture it, if we picture it as
oriental and populous and confined. Sefrou is a patch of fertile,

humid earth, alive with the gurgle of water. The pomegranate grove flames, the cherry swells, the fig tree has the odour of milk, the grass yields its juices as we bruise it. The Bengal rose masters the vine, a playful breeze whitens the orchards as it turns over every leaf at once. A place so pleasant makes man amiable; the *glaçons* are beautiful, the eyes and teeth of the young Jews gleam, water surges under the bridge between rocks and the terraces where corn and wheat flow like golden sands as the children turn them.

A rural Pasha governs this minor Eden of eighty hectares. He is going grey, he has a pugnacious nose between gentle eyes. He has fought loyally and well, as fond of the rifle as he is of the grafting-knife. Yet another who would like to cut Abd-el-Krim down to size; only give him two thousand horsemen and it would be all over. His house is cool, neat, simple, save for the beds reserved for lying-in-state; and when he takes us through the streets everyone kisses his shoulder. The enchanting rose garden in the square is not his, but he forces the lock to gain access, white and assured as a marauding angel, and gathers roses for us.

We leave to the sound of the springs that descend the slopes, that pass beneath the road, reappear to fill a green basin, and recross the road above our heads in a hollow tunnel that drips threads of quivering water and irrigates each vine-row, each barley-furrow. Happy spot, where plump children play and great snakes, plump also, quietly enlace the boles of the olive trees.

A Moroccan Luncheon

'Azil!'

Si-Kassem never had to call twice. She stood beside the door, leaning her shoulder on its cedar frame. She ran on bare feet with heels and nails of a dusky pink. She ran with her skirt in great folds, sprigged with white muslin embroidered with small flowers. Each time she brought a new offering : a straw pagoda, tented with velvet and braided with gold, sheltering round loaves of pure wheat flavoured with aniseed; covered dishes of red clay with a conical lid pierced by a smoking chimney, or perhaps some ewers. The ewer for washing and its copper basin, made in Fez, chiselled in rich yellow metal; the English ewer lined with silvered glass, from whose insulating walls poured bluish water from a spring that welled up from the ground a few yards away. There were six of us, seated in Turkish style round the low table. None of us drank from the contents of the water carafe during the meal; we knew that merely rinsing the mouth would preserve our appetite for a good Moroccan meal that we had learned to appreciate. . . .

'Azil !'

A silken scarf, modelled like a Parisian hat, revealed nothing of her hair. Azil was young and zealous and did not allow herself to smile. Her soft cheeks and bare round arms captured the blue from without whenever she passed the bay-window opening on to the sea. Azil mirrored the blue of the sky, the green of foliage; from each ear a glass pendant swung to its own bluish reflection on her strong neck. Azil was beautiful like a polished jar, beautiful like a young seal, beautiful like any well-treated, well-fed, sixteen-year-old slave.

She had already placed before us pale girdle-cakes soaked in sugared butter and sprinkled with almonds; pigeons bathed in succulent juice with green olives, chick-peas melting in flour, sweet onions; chickens buried under fresh beans with wrinkled skins and lemon cooked and re-cooked and reduced to a savoury puree. We had also had mutton, and mutton again, and once more; mutton stuffed with fennel, mutton with cumin and courgettes, mutton with twenty spices; and an exquisite diversion —girdle-cakes flaky to the limit of flakiness, rendered transparent, concealing a soft nugget of minced fowl, sugared and flavoured with nutmeg.

So what about all this sugar in dishes we customarily salt? Allow me to insert a laudatory parenthesis. Good Moroccan cooking—and I have perfect native hospitality in mind—has its secretly tried principles. It relies extensively on various dishes cooked on damped-down fires, in which—thanks to olive-oil—no one notices the lack of butter. As for the use of sugar in the main dishes, let me for a moment leave my Moroccan meal and slily select a recipe from one of the best manuals of French cuisine, a little volume published in 1839. I choose, from a hundred others, a recipe for 'shoulders of mutton *en musette*' :

'Remove all the bones from two shoulders of mutton and halve them; put the shoulders together, season inside with salt, pepper and fine spices; truss; lard the outer parts, coat with a layer of cooked forcemeat, *sugar the whole as desired*. Garnish with gherkins and truffles, lightly embedded in the forcemeat. Leave to cook in a braising-pan with a little ham, cover with slices of fat bacon and grease-proof paper, leave to cook on a slow fire. . . .'

I omit the details of glazing and dressing, which end with this ambiguous recommendation : 'It is advisable to cover with a full-bodied Spaniard or a reduced Italian', and return to the surroundings of Tangiers. But not without repeating that 'sugar as desired' recurs in many an ancient recipe for braised and stewed meats, and that sugar is indispensable for any dish that takes more than an hour to cook. There is no question of sugaring your purple steak or blue cutlet, of which I partake only rarely.

Ceaselessly Azil fetched and carried the red bowls. The spring vegetables took pride of place—broad beans, asparagus, new peas in a pot decorated with orange-trees, artichokes round as roses; small turnips, marrows and carrots appeared under swelling yellow enamel, with whole eggs broken over the dish a quarter of an hour before serving. Finally came couscous, at once soft and granular—couscous, discreet harbinger of desert and fruit—couscous with a surrounding rampart, a small fortress, of sweet onions and muscat grapes swollen to the sweating-point, couscous and bowls of barely soured buttermilk. We lifted our heads, we began to look at the sea, beyond an abyss of greenery tumbling to the shore.

They have vagabond, noble, disinterested souls who commit themselves to a motionless siesta on divans stuffed with fine wool and contemplate the Mediterranean through half-closed eyes. Already we can hear the water simmering in the bowls of the samovar. Faithful to tradition, our host rises to prepare the green mint tea. And if, simultaneously, we all turn to watch Azil of the black and pink feet, it is not because she seems more beautiful as she runs unburdened, it is because she is bringing to our host— oh, that odour that touches the throat with an iced finger, which plumbs the depths of the lungs, tells of snow and subtle pepper, wakens the spirits and deludes thirst!—a green bunch of crinkled mint.

Dar-el-Jamai

A terrace where blue and green enamel crumbles underfoot; a marble basin where a shred of water hangs always on one side, throbbing and fraying with the jetting of the source; the pink almond tree, the daturas whose long flower hides another flower within; the lizard studded with green turquoises, a long black tongue outside its mouth like a garden-lover sucking a blade of grass; a wild tortoise and a tame one that's always trying to scramble out of the water. But if you rescue it, it immediately attempts suicide head-first into the basin. The flower perfumes are all of a heavy cloying kind, winning their way by coarse means. Some await the night to overwhelm us—the datura, white tobacco, yellow broom. But the orange-tree never rests and takes the zest from one's midday appetite. But the honeysuckle and the fragrant oleaster reach the stillest corner at all times. A tree, whose name I don't know, dangles day and night a flower-bell from which descends an endless stream, a wave of odour in which I recognize the overripe apricot, crystallized strawberry, the fading lily of the valley, the tuberose and the rose when it begins to rot.

Full moon over Fez, a great bright moon of silver tinged with pink like the snow that gleams on the Atlas. Is it night already then? One had not thought so. With the night comes a deepening of the green on the slopes where Fez slides into the hollow of its valley; the deeper redness of a shawl and a burnous clinging to the steps of the old cemetery, while a long river of copper torn from the sunset stretches over the barley.

It is night, come as a pageant and presided over by the rainbow. The full round moon, elsewhere dragging up the tide, absorbs what's left of pallor over Fez, takes suck from this hollowed breast where the last shrill mixed cries of children and swallows now submerge, now uncover the uneven beating of a distant drum: Our European curiosity has already deserted us. What point in leaving this belvedere? The secret streets of Fez— secret? Perhaps the secret of this city is that it has no secrets. Everything it seems to hide fascinates : high walls of pinkish clay, closed doors whose two rings—one at a horseman's height, the other for the passer-by—strike the nail-studded door; captive gardens, inaccessible, guessed at, which display their young leaves and flowers at the top of their prisons. Whenever one of these doors opens it is to disappoint : a sulky, snuffly child gazes silently; a woman with reddened heels is washing linen; a suffering donkey waits, feet in its own excrement. That low dark threshold, polished with dirt, a hovel suggesting horrors to our romantic naïvety—but no, a man weaves in the shadow, thrusting his pointed shuttle on its path between the threads like a live fish. Or perhaps a tailor, with delicate hands and sick eyes, fastens together the folds of a djellabah, making a pretty stitch with smooth silk as a braid. Between the closed doors, the too-high walls, along the stifling streets where my outstretched arms touch both walls, we return in imagination to those recent times when the blameless traveller who ventured into the half-roofed alleys below the Jamai Palace risked an encounter with a well-placed blade.

From the height of the Jamai we can see it all—everything that matters: the hollow of Fez with its raised borders, its minarets, its conglomerated rectangles, its morning whiteness, its rust-coloured evenings, its blue-white sky like the sky that mirrors the sands, its confused murmur pierced by sudden cries—and the Atlas Mountains.

From this height we experienced only the flower of such a fine estate. In the evening, at the call of the muezzins, a bouquet of women erupts spontaneously over the terraces and an etherealized, insubstantial Fez climbs up to us.

The Pasha's Audience

It is thus that God the Father dispenses justice—if he exists. Also, He is handsome, vast, good, robust, ancient, ageless and majestic. Also He judges the poor. At the Last Judgment He, too, will say to the trembling bundle of rags, collapsed to kiss the ground :

La Chatte watching Colette at work

Colette and Maurice Goudeket in their apartment at the Palais-Royal

'I pardon you for having stolen that small handful of beans from a garden, for you might well have been hungry.'

But the Pasha detains—by the hand of the Avenging Angel, armed with a rod, huge, sombre, carrying the culprits suspended by the hair from his indifferent wrist—he detains the other thief :

'You have stolen beans and been caught selling them. So you did not steal from necessity. You will meditate on your crime in prison for two days.'

At intervals the Pasha sniffs delicately, as if his subtle nostril could detect the odours of innocence accused and crime concealed. Four arms-smugglers, prostrated at his feet (clad in soft wool), deny having sold the Rif a quantity of rifles. Three of the traffickers stay silent, leaving the fourth as spokesman, a grinning bewildered Arab unmoved by the white majesty of the Pasha or the clairvoyance of the French assessor (Captain T.), who acts as a public servant. The Arab, the colour of Fez clay, talks raspingly, using the whole linguistic gamut of adroit, eloquent Arab hands. The consignment of arms had been spotted in Marrakesh and in Fez and had then melted away to the North like a dream.

'No proof,' said the Pasha, 'but it was no business of any of you to peddle rifles. Get back to your own tribes down in the Souss. And don't enter the city gates again.'

He listens unmoved to the rising protests from the prostrate djellabahs. Squatting in oriental fashion, his back against an ordinary plank, he is radiant, silver-bearded, draped in light-coloured wool, with luminous great blue eyes showing where some blood alliance has disturbed the Arab night.

'You were drunk,' he says to a young man. 'Twenty-five francs for the crime of drunkenness.'

'I wasn't drinking,' shrills the accused Moroccan, dressed like a Frenchman in a dirty overcoat.

P.—D

The Pasha extends a delicate hand towards the Angel:
'Smell him.'

The Angel seizes the red-capped head and throws it back, then bends his scimitar of a nose over the anxiously open mouth.

'He stinks of it!' declared the Angel.

He smells. He must pay.

Now it's the turn of the mad mystic.

The madman stands with his tall dry body silhouetted against the light, reminiscent in his rags of the first Crusade. He is burdened with thirty wooden rosaries, from his neck down to his mud-encrusted feet, each bead larger than a plover's egg. Under his red hat his hair and beard are pale with ancient dust and he brandishes 'the spear of St John'. At Marrakesh he has been stealing, provoking scandal and pricking Jewish backsides. Marrakesh expelled him and he's been seen on every track between Marrakesh and Fez among the marigolds, the wild arums, the poppies and bluets; charged, according to him, with a divine mission, the madman—perhaps I should say the Holy Man—continued to pierce the backsides of Jews. Fez has received him on condition that he attends the Pasha's audience twice a month to answer for his conduct.

'What have you been up to?' asks the snow-white Pasha.

'Nothing.'

'You have pricked the backsides of Jews.'

'That is my mission.'

A few days in prison suffice.

But the wild figure stirs excitedly, the thirty wooden necklaces clattering in a halo of reddish dust. The Holy Man wishes to speak, if only to anathematize us all.

'I . . . I should like to see my wife,' moans the missionary hollowly.

'Your wife is in Marrakesh,' answers the Pasha, 'and, besides, you are a Holy Man and have no need of a wife.'

'It's true that I am holy. But it's precisely the want of a woman that threatens to annul my holiness.'

He turns his head and his dusty mop of hair from side to side and his great blank eyes search for Jewish backsides.

Here, kissing the ground side by side, are a sorcerer and a disgruntled husband. The pale, tormented husband alleges that the sorcerer promised to tell his wife's fortune. But first the wife had to hand over her jewels to him—the trouble is that the sorcerer kept them. The tale drags on with fluttering manual commentary. Gradually the sorcerer, at first silent and disdainful, begins to laugh in a manner showing him to be a true sorcerer, a laugh that reveals square white teeth, a conquering, impudent, irresistible laugh. What a delightful sorcerer! Even the presence of his own wife, whining, snuffling, veiled, does not make him at all downcast. Then Zeineb, too, accuses her sorcerer husband :

'Yes, he's a sorcerer all right ! Yes, he stole the jewels ! And he slept with the plaintiff's wife, and so-and-so's wife, and another's, and this Hanoum and that Hanoum. . . .'

What do I hear? French names ! The sorcerer laughs more than ever. And when he laughs his eyes—almost closed—show caressing and ironic between curved eyelashes; two shiny curling locks of hair shadow his cheeks; under his djellabah there is a gleam of white linen—it's obvious that he's a sorcerer, a sorcerer, a sorcerer !

The Pasha motions Zeineb to silence.

'If I am to adjudicate wisely in all this I must concern myself only with the matter of the jewel theft. For the rest is nothing but women's gossip and to take account of that would make one dizzy. Remove this Zeineb and bring me the black slave who took the jewels to the sorcerer.'

During the ensuing pause the just Pasha rests his gaze momentarily on the roses in the courtyard. A cool breeze stirs the long pendants of datura flowers. Flowers, clouds, untamed birds, these are the friends of this wise and powerful man who passed his youth far from the city, shared the wild tribal life and regrets the peace of boundless horizons. He seems to sail like a summer cloud on his bank of folded carpets. But it was a horse which felt the weight of this body filled with a noble spirit, when the Pasha left last year, at the age of sixty-nine, to bring back to Fez, to us, to France, the disaffected tribesmen who spread like an uncertain wave. He brought them back, after combat, pardoned and punished; and, as his horse galloped joyfully, two baskets of severed rebel heads swung from his saddle.

In Burgundy

A hard winter has prolonged its slumber. To the ignorant passer-by the vine still appears asleep. The vineyards of the Côte d'Or, stripped and bare, reveal their strict alignment, their fine disciplined framework. But something already quickens in the soil; and the same power that opens the bunches of red petals and the yellow disc of the first dandelions, that unwinds the caterpillars of the hazel and the honeyed catkins of the willow, this same sovereign power draws out on the wood of the vine a pointed bud, turgid with a tear of sap. Life stirs already on these resonant Nuits slopes; human hands and thoughts warm these precious plots, which bear witness to Man's long concern.

Several months must still pass before the peach tree blossoms pink, before the still mist of flowering plums whitens the hilly countryside on every hand. . . . The vine rests, but the *marque*[1] is at work.

Under the arches of the vaults, under the sparkling saltpetre, under the long stalactites of spiders webs, the *marque* works in the warmth, the mild warmth of a constant 13° Centigrade. Come the summer, and the same 13° will change the cellars into ice-houses in contrast.

We descend to the underground kingdom. A very fine blue mist—the casks have been sulphured—thickens the air under vaults starred with electric light bulbs. As far as the eye can see, as in the endless perspectives created in dreams, the walls are lined with barrels—barrels and yet more barrels. If we sound them with a knuckled finger in passing they all sing out that they are tightly closed and full of Burgundian wine. But each answers in its own way, each sounds like the note of a muted, distant xylophone. I recall the boastful words of the Pasha of Marrakesh: 'If I were to open my cisterns of olive oil, the river that flowed out would reach the sea.' Here, too, a river is kept imprisoned, a river of wine, a renewed store that time does not exhaust. Here one conserves for the present and the future, strives to preserve— perhaps one should rather say endure.

Is the antagonism that once ranged Champagne against champagne now going to range Burgundy against burgundy? It's an odd struggle and an old one, between the *cru*[2] and the *marque*. The *cru* is strictly defined and stubborn in its pride of race and its proper role: 'I am the pure stock', it claims. 'I have founded more than an empire. The mere mention of my name makes eyes shine, lips moisten. I have names sweeter to the ear than words of love, sonorous as war-cries. Even if I suffer anaemic crises or years of drought or rain, I alone possess the noble Burgundian blood!' Like all legitimate strains, the *cru* has its partisans, its pledged legislators, a blind commonalty and a terrible pride.

Today we are visiting a dissident who affronts the *cru*, a firm that sells only Burgundian wines: 'Analyse me, taste me,' they say. 'My wines wear the classic gold and ruby, they are free from bad breeding. I care nothing for the sun's caprices and unforeseen droughts. I gather wines from the Burgundian slopes. I blend the faithful scattered cadets that the *cru*, so long as it does not make use of them, stigmatizes as unworthy bastards. . . .'

As you see, I interpret, I sum up, in somewhat lyrical terms. But how can one speak unemotionally when it is a matter of national glory, of the wine of Burgundy? You may be sure the champions are no less lyrical than I when they defend their personal faith. It is in the name of the psychology of taste and the cult of healthy, sensitive, living wine that one cherishes and ripens this glorious wine in these cellars. In the cellars I am proudly shown a dusty 'library', rows of flasks for the storage of the standard types of wine, the consumer's elect.

It is a pleasure to be taught under the vaults where one's voice is subdued and one's footfall barely heard on the gravel. Work goes on everywhere, but the rhythm of labour is suited to the convenience of the wine, which dislikes both haste and roughness.

Around us on every hand, sounds are muffled. Here are the supreme quiet and luxury, soon to be denied us, of measured reflective rhythm. Outside, even the north wind gallops, the roads are thronged with cars, the telephones ring ceaselessly. But in this cloistered nursery of wine time slumbers and perhaps for a moment we cease to grow old. . . .

The men, wrapped in black aprons, are gentle and speak rarely. One of them, who racks the wine for the 'fining', bends over what sounds like a spring; and the perfumed odour of a young white wine, already fortified, mounts to the nostrils, whets the appetite and lightly intoxicates. The silver cup, for Our Lord of Wine demands silver plate, concentrates in its bright metal the small light of a candle. Uninterruptedly the filled cup passes from the tap of the cask to the face of the bending man; he touches it with his lips, swirls the contents round and looks through them at the flutings and bosses of the carved cup, empties them into a second cask, refills the cup at the first, starts all over again. . . . He stops. His expert eye has discerned the earliest cloud of lees where I still see nothing but limpid gold. . . . Only constant practice repeated over the years can so refine human sensibility. By his side a colleague 'dandles' the wine. Don't you love this earthy word, the picture it evokes? To dandle wine, in Burgundy, means to agitate it so as to clear it after the addition of egg white to attract and precipitate the impurities of a new wine. The man in the black apron, a true rosy Burgundian, agitates the *dodine*, a sort of iron boomerang curved at an obtuse angle, the curve always the same. As the instrument's name suggests, the movement is a rocking one, rhythmic and unhurried. The superiority of the hand! Living, sensitive, susceptible, the wine is a partner to the friendly hand. Are not the casks here still cleaned out *à la chaîne*? A heavy chain with thick round links scours the interior of the casks marvellously well, if the man who spins the barrel on its base only has the knack. Rounded, slow, immemorial manoeuvres, functions of the sphere and the circumference, modelled and inspired by the rotation of the planet. . . .

In the depths of the earth, in the bottle-filled cellar, rest the fruits of so much care; smooth young bottles, dated flasks, hoary elders, grey and white like the down that quivers on the bodies of night moths. . . . The master of ceremonies uncorks one of these. It is a moment for silence, for raising a swelling narrow-mouthed glass towards the vault; the eye first, then the nose, the mouth last. . . . Blessed be the. . . .

But, in fact, what can you call it, this velvet, this flame, this nectar, perfect in every proportion, full of afterthoughts?

One name, beneath the vaults, rolls and evokes the Burgundian r's which have stayed in my throat for half a century.

My Poor Burgundy

Can my birthplace, Puisaye, that used to be so thickly wooded, be reckoned as part of Burgundy? The least we Poyaudins and Forterrats claim is the right to call ourselves 'Low Burgundians' (coming from Basse-Bourgogne). When I was little, Forterre and Puisaye were two poor regions chiefly exploited by charcoal-burners, experts at constructing the fine stacks where the charcoal was made in a banked fire. A wisp of blue smoke rose from each secretly burning dome in the moist dawn air. Then the wind got up and broke the middle of the thread before dissolving it into mist. . . .

Hemp, too, was prolific, in enclosures bounded by green hedges. Its sweetish soporific odour made the children drowsy, sitting in the shade of the tall stems bearing seed that the birds pillaged. In sandpits there flourished the red-globed heather and the blue juniper. But my childhood holds no recollection of grapes. My Burgundy has hardly any vines, I admit it for truth's sake. In the Treigny district a light wine, a pretty ruby in colour with a tinge of mauve, did not resist the phylloxera.

The vein that bears the famous growths passes well away from Puisaye, divides and peters out. No vine-branches above my cradle unless it was some vine climbing a wall, some dense arbour beneath which the overshadowed bunches are thin and

105

etiolated and ripen only when the late season is scorching. Torrid autumn days are not uncommon in Auxerre. The soil can claim to be truly Burgundian; and the harsh sunlight and keen frosts that make for the great wines of the Côte-d'Or extend as far as our Puisaye.

Though devoid of vines, my home country drank wine. The little anonymous burgundy flowed there in bottles, in *setiers*[1] and *demi-setiers*, in *verrinées*[2]. It made its presence and its preference known on wooden tables marked by the bottoms of glasses with indelible purplish rings. On winter nights the young wine—at six sous the litre—bubbled in full mugs and in its pure foam there danced the slice of lemon and floating cinnamon, mixed with the ten peppercorns and rafts of shipwrecked toast.

Is it because of the wine at six sous the litre that reverence and confidence take root? No. It's always love that decides everything. The marvellous vitality of childhood memory amassed within me a solid castle of souvenirs: winter caterwauling, the noisy crackling of logs, the jets of blue gas we used to call 'wood farts', the scent of rubbed garlic—a Burgundian consumes as much or more garlic than a Provençal; each of my senses, adorned with rural poesy and fostered by the lyricism of wine, conspired to make out of a daughter of Puisaye the very acceptable Burgundian I now am. What the wine by the litre lacked in perfection I found in the paternal cellar. Our rocky slope guarded safely the stocks of choice wine built up by my father. My mother, after two fingers of Chambertin, would have fiery cheeks and push away her half-filled glass. It's amusing to think how, sitting on the broken rock, I worked harder than my parents at enjoying the wine-cellar. I drank wine every day, in very small amounts, savouring the mouthful in passing, disdaining at mealtimes the fresh water which 'turns into a frog' and bumps about as a heavy pocket in the stomach. My goblet of thick glass was small enough for me to drain it, large enough to satisfy me.

I was past my first youth when I came to Dijon, aflame with vines, and Beaune, where the wine goes underground to the song of the casks. For a long time I was content with those gifts of my poor soil that were freely given : chestnut and apple, the service-berry that is eaten over-ripe like the medlar, the red crab-apple that belongs to everyone, the damson from which the *eau-de-vie* gets its delicate flavour. And to think I nearly forgot the *courgelle*! Some call it the cornel-berry. It falls, ripe, in the month of August, stains the earth scarlet, is used for jam, and the children eat what's left over. . . .

Wild fruits, berries sweet or bitter, manna of a region with few resources, I hope you have not abandoned my pool-glowing Puisaye. Half a century ago I was more concerned to discover a spring, to dig up the grey truffle, odorous when raw but insipid after cooking, to contemplate silently the glossy back of a pheasant on her eggs, than to go in Sunday best to spend a week in Paris. Paris seemed to me closer, more intelligible, than the unknown Côte-d'Or. With the latter, it was a case of love, late but fierce, at first sight. My first stay there found me in the middle of reddening September, among the hillsides laden with their harvest, in a Dijon alight with a local feast, the end-of-season heat and the merry-making, unashamed either of being rich or of lavishing its treasure on a city devoted to gastronomic delight, running inexhaustibly with wine.

His Lordship, the Wine of Burgundy, paraded in the silver cup, in the footed glass and the goblet, reddened the deep shade of the vaults, the flowered napery and the tables of the inns. He listened to official discourses and to fireworks; he dripped in the hot dust under tents at fairs, gave his powerful aid to the crusted pâtés and the leg-of-mutton with garlic. . . . For three days he did not leave me and made of me his chosen victim, a rather too willing victim. . . .

It's because of those three days that, later, I wanted to see as a contrast the Burgundian vines in that ambiguous period when spring is still only a date, a rustling, a brief phrase improvised by the blackbird. The vine seemed asleep, skeletal, severely aligned. On its woodstock the bud had not yet changed its shape. A little old snow clung to the cold sides of the paths, but the first dandelions were in bud, the hazel catkins hung expectantly, the night frosts seemed to have scorched the couch-grass. Who would have thought that an outburst was incubating? I did not think about spring's explosion. I found it pleasing that, austere and shrunken, the Burgundy of the famous growths should resemble so closely, in its hummocky nudity, that other Burgundy, my poor, well-loved Burgundy.

The House by the Forest

Everything one says about a forest is true, or becomes true. But it must be a very big forest, large enough to enclose again within itself at dawn its nocturnal secrets, the patrols of wild animals that trespass beyond its confines during the night. It must be large enough to hide its lakes, shelter its herds of deer, continually astonish its poachers, affirm the reality of its particular spectres. Thus it is with the forest that encloses Rambouillet. With tracks in every direction, browsed in, patterned with crossways and signposts, it can still lead us astray if weather and season permit. It dissolves into mist, fragments into shards of rain, covers its pines and hollies unrecognizably under a mantle of snow; and we may feel, at any moment, that at the end of a tunnel of trees, beneath undergrowth rounded in a Roman arch, there stands a silhouette on two feet, or on four legs, and that it fades away as soon as it has appeared. . . . Might we have caught up with it on horseback? Nothing is certain. The untrodden path is green with smooth grass, the fine forest turf retains no imprint . . . it's just another ghost that has passed.

I am grateful now for all the mishaps that prevented me from furthering my acquaintance with the forest of Rambouillet: laziness, age, a tendency to procrastinate, and also the pleasure I had in staying—too briefly—on one of those gentle heights

above a pretty little town, behind thicketed ramparts. The paths
that intersect up there continue to the nearby forest. But, with
the exception of the ritual annual gathering—not to be overlooked or left too late—of anemone and wild hyacinth, lily-of-
the-valley, strawberry and foxglove, I followed with my gaze only
those charming ochre paths, crunching underfoot, that lead to
the lakes, to secret heaths, spongy dells, underwood sheeted with
invading arums.

For some thirty kilometres around there was nothing I didn't
know about their meanderings, their twists and turns. I knew
where they ended in some enchanted spot, an oasis of birch trees
with their slender shadows falling on sonorous gritty soil that
soaks away the rain and shines in the sun like a cracked window-
pane. Friable, sweet-smelling earth, grateful to the bare foot,
earth that the townspeople bundle up in a handkerchief to spread
as a panacea on the pot of nasturtiums or trough of pale
begonias. . . .

It was a house that used to keep me away from the nearby
forest and called to me when I was back in Paris. It is a favourite
error to suppose that a short distance is of no account when it
separates us from a place whose charm we keenly feel. It's no
longer convenient to live in Saint-Cloud or Montfort-L'Amaury
when one's work is centred in Paris. Even the best motor-cars
provide no real remedy, the contrary in fact. I find myself in
agreement with Monsieur de La Palisse; there is only one way
to live in the country and that is to retire there.

I have found that it is difficult, even illusory, to strike a balance
between working in Paris and the rural diversion that is supposed
to follow every evening, or every Saturday evening. Because of
my laziness—or because I am too broken-in to work—I have
never found myself able to feel free just because I was among
the fields. I haven't been able to forget them on returning to
Paris when some fine morning continues, without me, over the

rounded eminence of the forest, passes without me into the glorious noontide of a fine day, declines toward a beautiful twilight and, far from any sight or sense of mine, clothes itself in the blue of night, greeted by the owl's screeching and the fluting of the toad under the threshold. I should have made a bad London bureaucrat, I was too disorganized.

Did the house by the forest justify such tensions? It was by no means like one of those flimsy structures that spring up around a national park, age rapidly and readily change hands. Two hectares, innocent of kitchen garden, surrounded it. In the spring the three colours of purple orchid, blue polygala and plum-smelling muscarii arrived quite simply, even in the meadows, before the tall marguerites and the buttercups. I had only to prune the garden's stunted roses, its straggling box trees. From the middle of one façade—there were two, at right angles—a charming unexpected ox-eye window looked out on the meadows between two pink-flowered sturdy round chestnuts. Where but in the Ile-de-France do they know best how to plant chestnuts, a shelter against the rain, an umbrella against the sun? Only the house in the Midi has the virtuosity to display its pair of plane trees and the dense mulberry trained in the shape of a wheel by means of a light framework concealed under its foliage.

The ox-eye, as I said, placidly contemplated the grass, the narrow grove that skirted the road where the fieldmice, potent allies of the moles, had so undermined the soil that now and again a tree would lean over, its crown weighing down on its denuded roots, and subside gracefully to die. . . .

Not far from the chestnuts sprang a growth of black-wooded plums. In the spring they held up in the air a mist of flowers which August transformed into honeyed plums. In good weather the house revealed at ground level small rooms redolent of contentment, retirement, wood fires. . . . I was soon moved by its dumb speech of welcome. I still have a small corner of my heart that is gripped by the hinges of a double door there. No matter that the door, the black straw hat, the oval benevolent window, made advances less coherent, less simple than I might have wished. Whence, from whom, came the house? What 'artistic' taste sullied, albeit skilfully, its authenticity? I used to say to it, when we were alone : 'Shift a little, turn on your foundation, and you'll save us, both of us, from the freezing north wind. There was room enough, why didn't your first architect think of it? Turn your round ox-eye towards the pleasure of the sunset, it needs to redden in the fires of the south. And let this hooded hearth serve us with warmth, flames and winter comfort, smoking as soon as I put a match to the wood-shavings there. . . . You have a well, crowned with toad-flax and potentilla; but June empties it and all summer we thirst in front of this flowered ornament. . . .

So, increasingly, I came to doubt those unknown hands which had sacrificed to decorativeness and grumbled words like 'pseudo-peasant' and 'suburban shepherd', even though the house by the forest gave me genuine pleasure. If I do not count to its credit the bustling of the tits, the familiarity of the wagtails, the constant swallows . . . the fact is that they were served first and furnished with nests when our own beds were yet unmade. For the tits, there were traditional nesting-boxes made of unpeeled birch, pierced by a round entry-hole. I had brought these from Auxerre, where they know how to house wild birds properly and mould clay to suit the swallows. One of the blue-tits watched us at work, my odd job man and I. It was just right. The marvellous creature, painted sky-blue accentuated with willow-green and jonquil-yellow, was patient enough to wait until the nesting-box was nailed to the trunk of a tree and the ladder taken away. She darted forward, clung vertically to the birch wood, hesitated momentarily to question the sky and our presence there. . . . Then she threw herself into the nest head first, came out, went in again, came out again, called to her mate. . . . I've never since had the opportunity to admire such an impetuosity of understanding, such a total acceptance of risk. . . . I was rewarded with all this on a hot May morning—for tits are late in mating and nesting—by the house by the forest, whose merits and charms I was prompt to acknowledge.

Lanes of fine yellow sand wound across the meadows, just for the sake of winding. A sand-pit was the generous supplier. But beneath the sand lay clay, which killed the so-called ornamental shrubs I planted there.

A son of the cat, aged about six weeks, disappeared one morning at the age when he used to allow himself to be astonished by everything, to try and catch flies by dabbing a paw on them, to glance sidelong at morning shadows and to make use of the yellow sand, profiting from his new experience of the cat-tray.

His disappearance threw the house by the forest into confusion. But the odd job man created the worst consternation by remarking that birds of prey—buzzards, sparrowhawks and honey-buzzards —did not differentiate between young rabbits and kittens, chickens or small game. We were silent, beset by funereal thoughts: the great buzzard planing above the air-currents with a floppy little cat, already almost dead, hanging from its claws . . . the buzzard's brood around a frightful feast. . . .

The next morning the little lost cat, back again and very much alive but shivering with cold, was whimpering under a spring downpour outside our closed door. We all ran, one in pyjamas, one in a long old-fashioned nightshirt, one in a tatty raincoat. . . . This is the end of the tale of the little cat, but not of its legend. Later on we sometimes used to say: 'The little cat, do you remember the little cat carried off by a buzzard . . .?' and, later still, 'That house at Seine-et-Oise, you remember it, where the honey-buzzards used to carry off all the little cats. . . .'

The biggest gap in the estate, the 'view' as we called it, faced north and gave us an horizon of roads, rows of poplars, and villages. The forest, still the same forest, cast on the overpopulated earth its great outline of changing shadow, like a cloud drifting over the sea. Cold northern colours tinged the lower margin of the sky and it was thence that came the first false dawn that presaged evening, the first vaporous liverwort-blue peculiar to the east alone. From the nearby forest there came to us the piercing cries of birds before they rest, and in a few moments the breached expanses of the forest changed from green to deepest blue.

It was the hour when the forest re-exerted its sway and captured all the mystery of the countryside. The house became a refuge again, a temporary encampment, detached from an amorphous bulk. If one of us should propose a stroll by the lakes before dinner the other would hesitate, tempted by the sadness of the hour, the last violet rays thrown like a scarf round the trunks of the pines, the last leap of a bream shattering unwrinkled water, the piercing cry of a surprised bird, the gallop—muffled on the moss and guessed rather than heard—of four hooves hastened by the night. . . . From experience we were wary of what a twilit forest can inflict upon intruders, the snare of a grassy ditch full of icy water, a voice that is silent as soon as it is heard, a step that stops when we stop, a pleasure rendered spine-chilling by the hour, and the almost funereal whiteness shed by the wild cherries.

The warmth and chill, the light and dark, that pervade a forest when it welcomes the night, will always surprise us by the strength with which they reject everything that was delightful throughout the day—a roof, a pleasing enchantment, a familiar refuge. Whenever we yielded to the twilight's appeal we returned escorted by a great variety of noises, anxious to catch up with those who were satisfied with the protection of the beech and the cheeping of the drowsy squirrels. Our recollections were of the human fear of dark night, the huge trees, the sharp young moon, the star reflected in a damp leaf like an eye down on the ground.

One must believe that the forest damp engenders a fever encouraging to thought; and we used to bring the forest into the house in the shape of one of those bits of rotten bark, white as bone and light as sponge, that filled my room with the odours of driftwood and mushroom and gleamed till daybreak on my table like a fistful of glow-worms.

Close as it was to the forest, I sometimes used to wish that it were closer still, so as to accentuate the night terrors, the gladness of daybreak, that this nearness inspired. But it was only a tiny little house which—while I had it—kept a rather false charm, a chill flank exposed to the north-east. No thoughts or wishes would make it slip down the slope to that verge where the great woods began. It's a long time since I lived there; but just because I've lost it I can still dream of it, see in the mind's eye those small walls against a stirring forest, and fill them with some fabulous content.

Le Désert de Retz[1]

One wing of the Chinese edifice has just fallen, the rest is crumbling. . . . Is intervention indicated? If so, it had better be soon. This is not a matter of my personal views on the Far Eastern war. Merely that I've just returned from Le Désert de Retz. Curiosity might have tempted me to Ermenonville to see the buildings of the Méréville château; but the appeal of Le Désert is greater than that of other remains of landscape gardening. Will its preservation, thanks to the leading architect Jean-Charles Moreux, be in time? Will it be possible to save this last witness to a pictorial and architectural fantasy that doted on ruins, ivy, the browsing goat and broken bridge, recreated the debris with new materials and deliberately damaged the tower? Devoted to loosening stairways, the rustic chapel and the dungeon, the site inspired by Hubert Robert succeeded through its floral planning and utilization of the lie of the land. At Retz it frames a strange Tuscan column, truncated from the first and with mutilated apex, which, in its novelty, acquired the name of the Broken Column. If the efforts of J.-C. Moreux bear fruit, expert hands will be needed to tend this laboriously constructed folly, the conceit of an anglomanic architect, expert at harp-playing and archery, Racine de Monville.

It is obvious that the Column, once inhabited, an edifice that

116

surrealism might envy, is crumbling; that the gracious Chinese mansion is going to subside into the centre of the lake like moist sugar, that its panels of fretted wood are yielding to the pressure of dog-rose and elder. Certainly, the rare spirit evidenced by such audacious architecture and the magnificent arrangement of specimen trees in the park are entitled to endure, to be preserved like any village church or urban monument. But having made the acquaintance of Le Désert on a stormy June day, I shudder to think of it altered, deprived of its excrescences, affronted by the glamour of its own renewal.

Trespassing across the 'No Entry' sign by an exit devoid of doors, I had passed the real boundary, a gaping entrance decorated with two pilasters—white stone dominoes subsiding and toppling, burdened with ivy that both crushed and sustained them.

I shall certainly never know what Le Désert is like in winter. Like some marine bay to which each side comes as a mirror, a landing-place, just enough green and blue water to cover the ooze, so the month of June imposes on Retz a high tide of vegetation, effaces the evidence of its indifferent and discouraged proprietors, transgresses hope, and completes the work of Racine de Monville who wanted the new to be obliterated and scaffolding to be centennial. There is no mowing or pruning at Retz. Few of us realize the vigour that informs vegetable life on a soil fed by the fall of deciduous leaves, the annual maceration of grass. The abundance at Retz is that of a dream, a fairy tale, an imaginary island.

The visitor's unease begins at the tottering pillars and their moribund 'defence'. From the very threshold, plant-life usurps mineral solidity in an exuberance more dense than seasons permit elsewhere. The grass has grown a yard high wherever the shadows of the trees have not subdued it. Under a still stormy sky, low and blue, its mature fermentation creates a formidable odour of fresh humus and decaying petals, clover, mint and privet, rather like the odour that lingers behind too florid burials. The perfume clings to us as we ascend the avenue, still passable to vehicles, guarded by trees with trunks like towers, heads sixty feet above the earth, a skirt of branches intact to the ground, trees whose austerity and cascades of fresh green astonish. For nearly all, thanks to the climate, send out suckers and spring up again from the soil. Where they are separate, an immense velvety glade reveals a valley, a pool of clear bright water; but the reeds advance. An upper lake is all reed-spears and iris blades, moist overgrown traps. . . .

No need of a guide to climb to the farmhouse collapsed under ensheathing roses and vines. From here the eye discerns the basic outline of Le Désert like a beautiful body under a heavy covering, the happy valley exploited by a courtier who happened to be a man of taste. Hilly, varied, open at its heart to the light and the trickling of water, pierced by avenues one only guesses at, white with variegated hollies and red with purple oaks, the estate is obscured only by its unrestrained vegetation. The rest is harmony, for the Broken Column is no more than a folly without a roof-span. Across its threshold the central stairway curves ingeniously, the rooms rotate round its axis, scattered oval chambers arranged without affectation. . . .

Some mental effort is required before we can discern, in the apartment of the Column, its original role as an elegant dwelling-place, gracious and diversified, blending with its rectangles the softness of its outer curve. Today, between its curving walls, one feels equally both pleasure and a proper apprehension. An armed prowler would not dare to spend the night here. He would appreciate no more than we do the jumbled furnishings, the dark curtain that only clings to the wall by two funereal folds. Like us, he would prefer to this unjustifiable and expressive curtain the flight of any well conducted bat. An ordinary malefactor does not object to finding a skeleton behind some cupboard door; but hardly a suspended chair, leaning over into space, that has given up calling for help. What is a frightened snake in comparison with the white eyes of an ancient serpent that stares at us, dead and cradled in its jar? How to persuade oneself, in this prison gloom, that a rosewood bedhead, a gaunt armchair, the debris of a sewing machine, are not malevolent?

The oval windows, fitting into deep recesses in the Column, are broken. Nothing can resist a growing plant. Before a shattered pane I dream of the moment when the glass yielded with a crash under the silent invasion of wistaria. These same stems, more than a century ago, first stifled the delicate aloes and Farnese acacias, and those *grenadilliers* that were not really *grenadiers*,[2] but the climbing passion-flower (*granadilla* in Spanish). Now the ivy, the wild vine with its downy flower that smells like mignonette, block the charming view at every window. Two vine-shoots, that seem to be animated by a vegetable hostility against man, stretch out such meaningful tendrils that I keep my distance; they may have seen me. . . .

The storm, ever more lowering, clings to the lake. But we make our way down to the waterside because of its murmuring, because of the slight shiver, because of the intelligible and reassuring nature of a spring. For the breached opening of the ice-house under its pyramidal tumulus, its hollowed silence, mean nothing to us; besides, the day declines. A twittering of birds announces the evening. And with it comes the wish to leave this place of the past to a sleep and decay that only the seasons can fill with life. A little longer, and Le Désert de Retz will be no more than a poem in the style of an epoch. And yet, may it not be a fine thing to preserve even a poem from an epoch?

An Earthly Paradise

In Normandy the chestnuts and the apple trees shed their flowers together, the week has been cold and windless, and round the trunk of every tree is spread a circular carpet of petals, here pale, there a bright pink. A wind high up barely disturbs the tops of the thickets, the tailored arbours, growths more than fifty years old dotted over the thick grass of a well planned park, barred by flowing streams and illuminated by a lake. The grass, which came on late this year, is all flowers; buttercups give way to round patches of speedwell, every flower the blue of a blue eye. It has taken many a lustrum to fling the foliage of the copper beeches, over which the light streams like water, twenty yards high in the air.

A light trotting of delicate hooves is heard pattering along a nearby avenue. Quite close to us a fawn-coloured mask thrusts a gap in the privet; the horns, the heavy eye, the shaggy ear of the antelope do not flinch from our gaze. Propelled by their long, vigorous thighs, two small kangaroos spring from the long grass and are across the meadow in three strides. They leap so far they seem slow, as if suspended in mid-air, giving us ample time to register the image of their aerial passage, the small forelimbs drawn up against the breast, a baby kangaroo with its soft muzzle outside the mother's pouch. . . .

Is that someone laughing in the tree over our heads? Green, with a scarlet patch on its head and flank, a parakeet mocks us. And to leave us in no doubt as to the sociability and raillery of our welcome, the gibbons burst out in noisy whistling, or modulated and powerful song.

Original Eden must have been like this enclosed place. There, instead of man, one saw the monkey with its long belly, its slightly hunched shoulders, its language of howls, whistles and whispers, its small neatly grouped incisors, its pretext of a head of hair, the golden eyes that know how to shed tears, the human shadow— enormous behind the gorilla, minute beside the little spider monkey. In Eden, just as at Clères,[1] there were dwarf gazelles, so delicate that they might smash themselves on the rocks, and herds of blond antelopes leaping four-footed across a stream, Numidian cranes of celestial grey and pink flamingoes interspersed with the pink tufts of peonies. . . . As at Clères, a cassowary, the first cassowary, clothed in tubular bristles, neither hair nor feather, emerged from a wild rose bush to demonstrate how, on its neck and brow, it retains a fine reflection of the first rainbow. . . .

I find it delightful that, at Clères, the cassowary is not at all interested in the herbivora. The kangaroos do not look at the singing gibbons leaping along from branch to branch. What better guarantee of peace than indifference? No one asked Eden's dove to kiss the eagle and the lamb did not seek the warmth of the lion's flank. Everyone constructs his own pleasing image of the Mesopotamian paradise, that is of fairyland. Mine could not dispense with the animals. And, when M. Jacques Rouché asked me to write a fairy *divertissement*, I made a point of giving the power of speech not only to the animals, but also to a familiar world emerging from silence through hallucination.

The well-wrapped teapot, the bulging armchair holding out

its arms, the dial-face of the clock, the Numbers that so torment the Child—I thought them worthy of replying to the noble Cats, of applauding the Fire in its dance and the melodious Princess. But I did not realize that my desired illusion, an inoffensive tale, the squeaking of the bat and the lament of injured trees, would receive the dazzling aid of Maurice Ravel. M. Jacques Rouché, whose honour it is to have initially proposed this cordial collaboration and who put forward Ravel's name, must himself have had some doubts; for the composer of *L'enfant et les sortilèges*[2] had been working in silence for four years under the blue night-stare of his Siamese cats. In fact, Ravel's closest friends did not foresee the outcome of this four-year silence, troubled by the war. No one guessed that, thanks to a little poem—I'd stupidly entitled it 'Diversion for My Daughter' until Ravel said, with icy seriousness, 'But I haven't got a daughter'—a great composer would leap beyond science and humour and speak with unsuspected sensitivity.

A late discovery, like almost all discoveries, the music of *L'enfant* brings tears to the eyes at the Opéra during the dance of the spells, embellished and humanized to excite laughter. The frogs croak and jump, the bats squeak, the dragonflies waltz. . . . The librettist had not envisaged, with her gay little piece of magic, that an orchestral outpouring starred with nightingales and fireflies would raise her modest offering to such a pitch. The return to commonsense of a wilful child, the reconciling murmur of animals become tutelary because they have been helped—how well I saw and experienced Ravel's tenderness singing in the wonderful final chorus, moistening the eye become oblivious to the scene. . . .

Thus it is that the chief begetter of a work gains his true place and empire. Giraudoux, with *Ondine*, relegates La Motte-Fouqué to second place and the fantasy designed to catch the eye has won the heart. It is a good omen that the surprised public approves of *L'enfant et les sortilèges*. Whatever is possible and may become true is something that doesn't yet exist, and which human reason dare not promise. *Ondine* is not the least real of stage heroines because she took so long to become amphibian. Henceforward, she exists within us until the day, a hundred times foretold, a hundred times imagined, when her formal existence as a water-nymph will no longer rest on the number of witnesses but on the faith she inspires.

At Clères, in the zoo park, it is easy to lose the melancholy feeling of inevitability. The owner of a magnificent park does not pretend to do more than acclimatize species brought from afar, and let them multiply, using the minimum of confinement. He is a man of science, a generous sportsman, fertile in curiosity. But he does not realize that some of his visitors are easily disturbed and prompt to obey the instincts roused by a cry intelligible in other latitudes, by a singularly-nailed footprint, by a backward-placed hand. To upset my conception of our hemisphere it is enough, for me, that at Clères, in the stifling green air of a hothouse where one of our common cabbage butterflies had slipped in, I've seen the humming-bird, weightless creature all wings and rubies, frightened by the butterfly almost bigger than itself.

Having recently witnessed the fire that destroyed the château but did not harm the animals, it may happen that the park at Clères displays to the everyday world, above its walls, a blue and purple feather, a bird from an Australian nest, that an antelope bars the way to a truck. I like to think that, in a Normandy wood, if I held up my hand to heaven, my arm would make a marvellous perch for such winged miracles as the lophophorus, the lace-capped goura, a hyacinth macaw, the Chinese pheasant in its golden armour. It would be the foretaste of something marvellous, the beginning of the approach to a door beyond which one would encounter—friendly and forgetful of his power, artless,

bearing his ineffable after-smile in his eyes, moving amidst the
windmill noise of his purring, the one considered inaccessible,
that unknown whom, under all his feline names, under all his
tawny robes, I recognize and name—the Cat.

La Treille Muscate I*

In order to find it I had to tear myself away from the little Mediterranean port, the tunny boats, the low houses painted a faded sugary pink, lavender-blue or lime-green, the streets filled with the odours of eviscerated melons, nougat and sea-urchins.

I found it by the side of a road that motor-cars avoided, and behind the most commonplace gateway—but this gate was strangled by oleanders urgent to extend to passers-by, between the bars, their powdery bouquets of Provençal dust, as white as flour, finer than pollen. . . .

Two hectares, vines, oranges, green- and black-fruited figs— if I add that garlic, pimentoes and aubergines filled the rows between the vine-stocks, haven't I said everything?

There's a house too; but this—small and low-storeyed—is less important than its open wistaria terrace, for instance, or the flaring red bignonias, or even the ancient thick-trunked mimosas drawn up in a row between gate and doorway. Behind the house . . . no, I can't see anything behind the house that really deserves description.

Behind the house are more vines, then a rampart of false bamboo, a yielding Provençal wall that takes the battering of the mistral, springs back and sings angrily. Behind the house the enclosing thuyas lean over a half-rotten fence and if you pass

through this fence, that a child could overturn, you go straight
into the sea without taking a step up or down.

I did, in fact, forget to mention that the sea borders, continues,
extends, ennobles, enchants this plot with its luminous shore, the
sea coloured or blanched, according to the hour, by the sun that
soars at dawn from the cold blue east to die at evening in a flurry
of long, straight, ominous pink clouds. It is the sea that provides
the vines with this friable salty soil that so mysteriously sustains
their stocks. It is the sea that has drawn me here. Here I am free,
now, to live if I wish, to die if I can . . . but we haven't got as
far as that yet. I've only just arrived and settled in. The musk-
vine arbour that endows the well with its name and covers it
with its shoots did not swell the taut, blue-reflecting bellies of its
grapes for me. The musk-vine arbour that I have bought is not
yet mine.

I must go carefully, and economically. A musk-vine arbour
isn't equipped in a single season, by grand provision of a stucco
bathtub, saffron walls and rustic pottery. I shall hurry to deal
with what's most urgent, that is the garden, then the room—if
I may so describe it—the outdoor bedroom. The house, that can
be left for the moment. This one has its meagre past, its modest
frontage that one would prefer more rustic, its household gods
smiling like old workers in the fields. That's enough to be going
on with. If in the end it takes after me it must be gradually; I
must fashion my place in it like a dog who turns round and round
to bed himself down in the straw. The largest room for hours of
idleness and conversation and reading, the smallest for writing in
—and we'll choose a rather dark one, not too comfortable,
removed from marine enchantments—it's a matter of plain
commonsense.

The garden, the garden; quick, the garden; but there's no
'garden', thank heaven: there are the tall yellow plumes that
brush the sky, the mimosas whence the perfumed pollen falls, we

shan't touch them, only to exact a reasonable toll. The morning-glories are already settled in their traditional place, against the hot front wall of the house.

We must respect the thatched porch-roof, sagging at the centre, we must respect the ancient *olea fragrans.* . . .

But between the ancient mimosas, on either side of the path, two low walls made of hollow bricks contain the vines, narrow the path. . . . To the devil with the brick walls! The wisdom of the vine-branches! Vines, you deserve slender iron pergolas, you really deserve that I should plant supports for you here and there at random, pillars for you to hang from, parasols where you may blossom and cascade. . . . Vines, you shall soar into the sky, you shall breathe the breeze that does not always brush the earth, the rough underside of your leaves shall relish the torrid vapour that summer sucks straight from the soil, and from your woody shoots, O vines, I shall build trees!

Lyricism or delirium? The Mediterranean shores have turned many a sound head. Over the pine-groves near the musk-vine arbour there passes a resin-laden breeze and the labiates of the coast distil camphor, essence of lavender and balm. My garden will be no less docile beneath its aerially-transformed vines. The tomato, fastened to stakes, will shine with a thousand globes, empurpled as June advances; see how many love-apples, violet aubergines and yellow pimentoes, grouped in an old-fashioned convex border, will enrich my kitchen-garden. . . . There, garden, there! Don't forget you're going to feed me. . . . I want you decorative, but full of culinary graces. I want you flower-filled, but not with those delicate flowers bleached by a single cricket-chirping summer's day. I want you to be green, but not with the relentless greenery of palms and cacti, the desolation of Monaco, that simulated Africa. Let the arbutus glow beside the

orange and the bougainvillaea's violet torches clothe my walls.
And let mint, tarragon and sage grow at their feet, tall enough
for the dangling hand to bruise their branches and release their
urgent perfumes. Tarragon, sage, mint, savory, burnet—opening
your pink flowers at noon, to close three hours later—truly I love
you for yourselves—but I shan't fail to call on you for salads
to go with boiled leg of mutton, to season sauces; I shall exploit
you. Down there I shall reserve all that I have of disinterested
botanic love for her—Her, the pride of every favoured clime—
Her—the Rose.

Don't ask me where I shall plant the white rose undone by a
puff of wind, the yellow rose smelling of fine cigars, the pink rose
that smells of roses, the red rose that dies without losing its
fragrance and whose dry light corpse still spreads its balm. I
shan't crucify that one against a wall, I shan't tie it to the edge
of the cistern. It shall grow, if my good angel permits, close to
the outdoor bedroom, the room with only three walls instead of
four that will face the rising sun. I can't promise that such a
room will even have a ceiling, unless it be of tangled roses. Last
summer I even dispensed with wattle. How many nature-lovers
are there who love her enough to spend the night in her bosom,
for love, for love alone . . .?

No mosquitoes here. Last summer I dragged a mattress and
blankets outside a little summer-house every evening and slept
with the mistral in my hair. Two faithful owls conversed in the
pines until midnight and the crackling brazier of the crickets fell
silent only after they did. You clammy sleepers, stifled between
hot walls, envy me! For the nights in this blazing country are
chill and the bodies of those who abandon themselves under their
stars are relaxed and cool, balanced between dream and blissful
unconsciousness. And what happy dream is worth the hour of
sleeplessness that gave me, a parting gift before daybreak, the
sleeping Mediterranean, lustreless, white presaging ultramarine

—the sky that brushed and overlaid it already bright and wide awake—the sky with its sad red seal slowly breaking at the edge of the world, slowly opening just as I fell back, satiated, in a dream world that my vigil saw as multicoloured, comparable to the wind in the sails of a ship as it gets under way. . . .

La Treille Muscate 1930

It has not broken faith. If I smile when I reread the lines it once inspired in me, it is not to ridicule either it or myself. It is because now it shows me its true likeness, just as a trusting wife in former times, the wedding-night once over, might display her fresh charms in night attire, her ringlets rolled round little twists of paper.

'O vine!' I declaimed to myself, 'I fling you into the air and you descend as creepers!' It's very touching, the lyricism of one's first encounter. I said much more. I spoke of a thicket of vine-stalks. A thicket of vine-stalks! One ties up the stalks while they are green, prunes them when dry and short if you please. The vigour of their sap is so powerful, their foliage so dense. . . . I spoke of 'rosary', of 'thickets', and even of 'ornamental vegetables' —as if they were going to wait for me to assign them an arbour of a terrace to become 'decorative'.

The first enthusiasm over, I summoned a guardian spirit of the locality, a dark attractive man with crisp hair and white teeth whose occupation was that of horticulturist. I was emphatic and free-spoken : 'I want you to. . . . Understand? There's no point in keeping this. . . . No geometry! Don't worry about straight lines . . .! Do you understand?'

130

He nodded his head. 'Yes . . . yes, actually I'd like. . . .' He paused for a long moment, then said in a tone of the blandest melancholy: 'It's just that it wouldn't be Provençal any more. . . .' He went on to add: 'As far as I'm concerned, it only suits me to work in proper Provençal style. . . .'

How easy surrender is in that part of the world. . . . Do not condemn me, my garden is charming. Idiot, to dream of rose thickets! Why not an English park? I think of my past plans as serious breaches of good manners. The intruder who disfigures this countryside does not thereby succeed in imposing himself on it. It is a very ancient land this, but uncouth, and it has made the native wary. He asks no more of it than it wants to give. He abandons to the vagaries of a climate that never ceases to astonish him the rock decked with wind and pines, the rubble where only cistus grows, the hillside that nurtures only grass and wild arbutus, wormwood, cactus, myrtle and lentiscus. And having, literally, gone through a fiery ritual, man ranges his stakes, plants cypresses in rows, spears of false bamboo, and puts his tentative blossoming plots in order. Frost nips them more than once in winter, summer often exhausts them if one rations their water. . . .

The guardian spirit, rough-haired as a cypress, instructed me how to design a 'proper Provençal' garden that would stand up to any challenge. I still questioned the wherefore of things:

'But this garden looks like a grid-iron! Why must you make the flower-beds all parallel?'

With unlimited patience the spirit condescendingly shakes his curly head, scattering seeds of wild millet, anemone petals, a mixture of tenses and imperfect subjunctives, relics of an ancient dialect. . . .

'Eh! How else should I manage? I only wish it was easy to change the direction. Why, only last year you made me plant the lilies the other way round and the month of August finished them off. See for yourself how you have to plant. . . . What is it settles the direction for us, anyway?'

His arm points to the sun and, descending, plots an immutable path in the sky from east to west. Sourly, I think of future market gardens, crammed tight. . . .

'So that's what it's like, a proper Provençal garden?'

'It's like that and it's not like that,' replied the spirit grandly. 'But it's begun well. Just be patient a little. . . .'

Half a lifetime may elapse before a tree casts on the earth the oval turning shadow of a perfect crown. . . . I can't wait all that time.

If, nevertheless, I plant a fig tree it's from tradition, in pagan reverence towards a sun that has always given birth to fig trees. I must give preference to whatever hastens to stretch out to the light, fill itself with water and sunlight, swell with buds, explode in corymbs and rosettes. To have to abandon the tree whose stock one has grafted, to abandon the shade where one cultivates a nursery, is possibly not the least bitter, the least keenly-felt form of resignation. . . .

Begun slowly, and in a small way, in 1926, the Provençal garden makes progress. It pleases me to think that it will never attain the fixed perfection of Mosaic ambition. Everything is against it, myself above all; it has to cope with unsuccessful experiments, seeds that are too old, the mistral, frosts. The hard winter of 1928–29 saw the destruction and death of the ancient mimosas, glory of the short avenue. Their enormous trunks, beautiful and glossy, split as if they were on the fire. The few eucalyptus trees that filled the night with their odour of tomcat and embrocation were killed by frost; an axe of ice inflicted mortal wounds on the heart of the ancient mulberries. . . .

Ill-fortune and vicissitudes have not prevented me from under-

standing, despite too much frustrated care, the essence of a
'proper Provençal garden'. To be frank, it's a garden that's like
all the other humble gardens I've known and made in the French
countryside. What else did I imagine? The garlic is at the foot
of the wall, the pepper by the rose-bush that's pruned hard back
to resist the wind. The aubergine and the tomato are traditionally
neighbours. I'm familiar with all that from childhood. Did I have
to come so far to regain what I'd left behind?

I question my familiar spirit, capped with a hairy black
parsley. He replies with only a gesture of the arm, the arm that
traced the sun's track in the sky. He points to this plot that so
much resembles the little market gardens of Grasse. He shows
how, in the foreground, marigolds tinted with the hues of wild
wallflowers and bees restrain a border of violet petunias, each
blazoned with a white star. Lilies flaunt themselves above the
petunias, their flowers rivalling in beauty and fleshy softness the
febrile tongues of orchids. The zinnias' domain starts at the
highest level. For years now the zinnias have been as large as
saucers, as cushions, like the round mats our grandmothers used
to embroider. They favour every shade save blue; and in mine
there predominates a pure red, a Chinese pink and another,
saffron, pink.

A thousand zinnias, and yet another thousand, tirelessly
preaching the glory of the flower that is perfectly round! One
more thin rank, behind and strictly parallel to the three foremost
—this is the narrow domain of the tall spiky amaranths, purple
mares' tails swayed by the breeze. . . .

Lastly, at the very summit, absorbing the sun and formed in
its image, reign the broad-faced sunflowers with their hearts of
black honeycomb. From their stiff stalks there hangs in rivulets
that incomparable flower, the blue convolvulus, darkened by the
passage of a cloud, opening and becoming blue again as the sun
returns. . . .

From June to October I have at hand this simple compact bank of flowers. None of them are rare. But an exceptional sky hangs over them. . . . Around the scarlet zinnias and the red geraniums there vibrates an indefinable violet halo. The yellow marigold exults in its confrontation with sky and sea, and the convolvulus. A lily, flesh-coloured and with thick pulp, bursts through the soil each morning, lifts its rigid calyx as high and as quickly as it can, with its heavy fragrance of bruised peaches. . . .

O light! The wall, from closeness to so many flames, blushes like a cheek. Now I know what a Provençal garden is; it is a garden that has only to flourish in Provence to surpass all others.

The fauna, however much one tries, remains feline. I don't count my bulldog as a dog. Neither does she. The ordinary dog here is the progeny of heaven-knows-whom, is of sickly growth and rendered gaunt and empty of intelligence and energy by the long summers. When the shade has reached the coast road, one hesitates to whistle to one of these floury phantoms lying in the white dust, who get up breathing a deep sigh, shake off their cloud, and begin a lagging trot as if to say: 'You can guess from my fatigue how devoted I am to you!'

The musk-vine arbour shelters two stray dogs, one an uncurled Restoration type, the other rather Louis XV as far as the paws are concerned, doubtless a souvenir of a neglected infancy. Both lead quiet lives, unburdened by care, except during nights of the full moon. Its ancient face torments them periodically, they swear at it and chase the phantasms it conjures up, while the lordly cats dance and enjoy themselves.

One, two, three, four . . . eleven cats. How many will there be next year? The swollen belly of a female promises a litter of six. Two grey tomcats strut on the wall before the brash grey female who was a suckling only three months ago. A bland, snake-grey cat, its cheeks puffed out like a small lioness, naïvely rehearses its wailing call under the spindle trees, the 'bird-call'. So many greys? Yes, so many greys. My South American pair—some say Russian—think nothing of three litters in twelve months. More than that, the tom, Krô, sows his silver-grey progeny, blue in shadow, far and wide. Dawn and twilight bring forth grey cats. A shed, a ruined wall, a trimmed hedge, each shelters its quota of grey cats, hardly altered by random matings. The pure strain, determined and transmitted by the females, is rather short, stocky, with a powerful neck in the male. Winter endows them with a thick, not very sleek, fur that distends their cheeks, shortens their ears, and makes them look like bear-cubs. They are less afraid of water than the ordinary French cat and stroll about in drizzle and showers, silvered over with the droplets held imprisoned in their fur.

Krô, Kapok, Muscat, Touteu-Petiteu, Pichinette, Minionne, Toune . . . and five others . . . and the one 'who's called Mini-Mini because he's got no name, poor thing!' At first sight you'd think them all alike. There aren't three of us who can recognize them at a glance. . . .

That long, gliding, supple stride, that joyless unfrank gaze, that's Kapok, the castrated male who beats the females.

Krô, as big as he, is still, at four years old, the Herculean child who will abandon his favourite plaything—a grain of rice—to kill a rival. The fierce battle over, Krô lowers his eyes before the female, sings to her in a tiny voice, and tolerates her sharp prudish cuffs. . . .

Toune has always lost something or someone, her plate, her cushion, her bowl, her ball of wool; but she is so pretty that she always finds someone to marry her—two or three times a year.

Darling Pichinette, Touteu-Petiteu who is the best of mothers and produces the most beautiful offspring in the world, Mini-Mini the nameless . . . grey, grey, grey and grey again. I grant those who haven't seen them born the right to get a bit fed up with them. But just stand watching on my doorstep, looking towards the vine and the small pine-wood, while I cry a certain cry, followed by a little song that has—for you—no meaning. In a moment you'll see her approaching, the one I have virtually summoned.

Slowly, so as not to reveal her affection too openly, slowly she advances on very small silver feet. She carries her head as she does her tail, both stately yet unconstrained. Her golden eyes smile softly because they have met my own; yet this perfect creature may assume a demonic appearance in passage on account of a grasshopper or a fresh molehill, and the regal procession gives way to a prodigious somersault. . . .

'What came over me then?' she reproaches herself as she lands. Three small steps, a leap in the air to avoid a branch, a stretch at an antelope's trot to show her zeal, a gentle dove's cooing and some feline utterance so that we may admire the healthy warm redness of her tongue; there stands before you, grey like all the other greys but one whom you won't confuse, having seen her once, with any other grey cat, she who rejects the names of queens, the childish diminutives, and is called—as if she were the only one in the world—Cat.

Finistère

The hotel, situated high beside the beach, has a romantic name. We came here by chance. A little road, then an isolated village, then a sandy way, then . . . nothing. The end of the world, the dramatic '*fin de terre*'. Sonorous, the sea begins to come in over the fine firm sand in rollers whose glacier colours can be seen through the foam. Two kilometres of unblemished beach, without a frond of seaweed, with no imprint but the marks of birds' feet. A gentle virgin slope to lead one down to the sea, astonished at such serendipity, surrounded by a kind of furious silence, the sound of an assault so uniform and so constant as to become negligible.

The shallow valley extends as two protective capes. The hotel dominates the bay, intrudes with its floral approaches. Having enjoyed the pleasures of a rapid bathe in cool weather, with the waves pounding one's neck, we'll try to get a hot drink. . . .

Within, the vast red-brick shelter is like a well-kept convent smelling of beeswax. A little Breton girl glides up silently, hair upswept, Quimperlais ribbons flying behind, raising her eyebrows as if we had roused her from a hundred years sleep. But the tea soon arrives, and sparkling cider, and hot golden pancakes, and perfect salt butter spurting pearly whey under the knife. . . . A Breton silence surrounds us, with the humming of the wind and the rising tide at its heart. Beyond the capes stretch more golden beaches, blue thistles, frothing waves, and solitude.

I turn towards the unwrinkled beach and try to picture children, women avid for a suntan. . . . Does France, then, still hold unknown beauty, accessible splendours? Look what it has granted this pair of travellers, this gentle Brittany of flying spindrift! Near Roscanvel, around Landévennec, the meadows are bordered by red and violet fuchsias, poplars and fig trees lean together over sea-water still a little milky and barely saline. Ten small sheltered ports are only flowers, greenery, invitations to leisure. On the other hand, this westernmost earth of France, weathered by great winds, offers a foothold in its smooth, pink Spanish soil only to the dwarf furze. The wild thyme grows in rounded patches. Lay your cheek on its springy flower, sleep in its dry perfume in the shelter of a rock; the dull thunder of the waves exploding under the cliff will lull you. . . .

I am grateful for a year, like this one, that keeps me almost sedentary but leaves me sensitive to the encounters of a mere six kilometre journey. A week in Finistère reminds me of the words of an English friend: 'I shall not be making any more long journeys; I have France.' It was this same honorary traveller who led me, wherever roads divided, to many a surprise, such as an unknown convent shunned by some dreadful casinos nearby; a mountain inn, standing on piles above some dizzy Mediterranean panorama of coasts, mountains and blue air. . . .

Here, between Camaret and Quimper, what better than to follow the roads with their capricious signs, often devoid of any directive indication? Pleasure and peregrination have become synonymous, we waste time only. Where the tourist fails to tread, Brittany seems to belong to us and all her delights are reserved for us, so true is it that speed has brought the straitjacket of itineraries and timetables, ineluctably spewing coach-loads of hotel-diners and peripatetics. . . . Solitaries like ourselves discover that a meal at an inn depends on solicitude, personal whim, not on haste and obligation. It may happen that the butter has just been beaten, that a fisherman has just caught this fine, fat pink-fleshed 'clenched fist'. 'I've a little cream as well,' announces the *patronne*, and her little boy gathers from the garden a bowl of strawberries not included in the menu. . . . Sometimes, even, a cook will grant us the favour of a little of her time, a little personal goodwill : 'Don't have the grilled sardines, I've got a quarter of an hour to make you my Lobster Mélanie. . . .'

Around Plougastel-Daoulas, between the hedges of fuchsia and honeysuckle, under the now heavy apples, silent children and young girls in their head-dresses hold out baskets of strawberries with a musky flavour. . . . Marvellous savours of France, perennial essence of fruit, race and countryside, how satisfying to maintain our loyalty by the most refined of our senses as well as by a stronger and more sensitive attachment ! Caught as we are in passage, evoked by some chance halt, Breton reserve and welcome and aloof pride suffice to vanquish us, intimately linked as they are to an ancient past, a faithfully observed tradition.

Now hastening, now idling, on the long humped back of a peninsula illuminated by the presence of the sea on either side, we run across a gathering in gala costume, a celebration that dispenses with tourists, shooting-galleries, lotteries and caramels. Behind an awning barring access to a field, a wrestling-match is the focus for a purely Breton crowd, among which we stand out. On the shaven grass two pairs of wrestlers in short linen breeches trample two sawdust rings. Their ancient Celtic sport calls for a kind of jacket of yellowish material, like a second skin that each grasps in handfuls on his opponent, just as bulldogs seize each other by their ample necks and dangling dewlaps. In addition, one is entitled to encircle the neck with an arm and to hook a leg around the other's leg and so topple him over. But the jacket is being continually pulled out of its belt and with well-nurtured patience the wrestlers adjust themselves, roll and unroll the long belt. Their movements follow each other without haste, victor and vanquished disentangle themselves and walk off in step, leaning against one another. Here, three kisses replace the traditional handshake before each bout, three resounding kisses on the cheek that can be heard in the quiet setting. How could one not hear them? The audience makes no sound, utters no cry. No applause, no booing.

The beautiful leafy horizon, the oaks—green to dark blue, the needle of grey granite that sounds the hour, the grouped men, their tall black hats banded with velvet and clasped behind with a massive silver buckle, the group of women—winged head-dresses with stiff muslin bows under the chin—no one moves or talks, one can distinguish the 'pink, pink' of a finch in the hedge. Plougastel-Daoulas is represented by its Renaissance bonnet, embroidered with pearls, and fastened with a slender throat-string, and its spangled apron. The dresses of Quimper are of black velvet cut with admirable precision; the triangle of the back, the sections under the arms, fit without a wrinkle, and the gathers of the skirts swell under flaunting aprons. Aprons of blue velvet fitted with spreading panels, the seams picked out with spangles; aprons of green satin with designs of red and violet flowers; gauze beaded in floral designs in grey, black and white. . . . What opulence! One young girl has composed her dress within a net of black chenille, another is dressed in patterned, fashioned, sheared velvet. . . . And what hair-styles—rolled up in a shell under the bonnet, braided into ropes, red, brown with golden strands, black as Chinese tresses! One blonde beauty is as silent and modest as the others in her demeanour. But she shows herself regal by her fine nose and downy cheek, and her incomparable hair, so black as to be almost green. Also, on her deep black dress with silvery folds she has tied an apron as pink as a fading rose, brilliant with purple flowers and dewy pearls. . . .

Now a wrestler falls, puts his shoulder out, faints silently. What shouts there would be if it involved a sporting crowd in Paris! Here he is carried off amid general indifference and those spectators who are seated don't even get to their feet. Only a young priest (dare one say factitiously) works himself into a sweat.

'I suppose,' my companion ventures, 'the accidents that occur in this kind of fighting are not very dangerous?'

The young priest, offended, calls him to account:

'Not very dangerous? These are very serious fights, sir! We've already had one death. The vertebrae of the neck fractured, sir! Indeed!'

He wipes his forehead, dashes off for news. But the blonde from Quimper does not spare a glance for the injured man. Nor the curly redhead of the fiery aureole, nor the golden-haired girl crowned with braids. Thus the princesses behaved, at the tourney. . . .

Discoveries

Why not regard the unusual as a luxury? It must be fifteen years since I last spent the month of August in Paris. This August is not too fierce. It's surprise enough that Paris no longer means crowds, movement, even work. I don't worry about going without others, they'll turn up again soon enough.

Apart from the insane, who become more cracked as the thermometer rises, Paris in summer still has the wherewithal to amuse its prisoners. But it no longer resounds to the same noises. The clamour of a storm, normally drowned in traffic and motor-horns, regains its importance, and its echoes, reminds us of the movement and the direction of the wind: 'That's passing over Rambouillet . . . Chantilly's getting it all right!' Insulated from hurry, from the sort of military compulsion that comes from green and red lights, double rows of studs and watchful police, it is pleasant to stroll with head thrown back and discover the wide ballooning sky, the blue threat of hail, a sudden silvery shower, the sun setting between two fiery rims and often, around six o'clock, a rainbow spanning the Seine above the Pont Royal.

A somnolence typical of avenues steals over the green places. Shall I soon be the only provincial lady on her yellow iron seat in the Tuileries? It's nearly come to that. The black-tongued chows, the cocker spaniels nursing incurable heartaches—have they conspired with the animated ball-players to absent themselves? That poor, handsome young man who used to eat his lunch astride a stone bench, biting into his bread with a kind of frenzy, has he, too, been able to leave Paris? It was my usual morning recreation to discover the habits and secrets of those who sit from noon to half-past one and lunch by themselves to hide the fact that they haven't much to eat. Between the borders of heliotropes and large yellow anthemis, behind the violent red of the geraniums, in the shade of opulent flowers and statues, one may discover those who are unwilling to face total loss and prefer to spend their free time among the relics of royal parks and houses. They only meet—we only meet—solemn children, forgotten in Paris by the summer, or eccentrics who have as yet committed no crimes and talk to the clouds. Half-past twelve . . . one o'clock . . . a quarter past one. . . . At La Rochelle or Lons-le-Saunier the shaded arcades are no more deserted or shuttered than those of the rue de Rivoli. I wonder who it is playing the piano up there, under a zinc-clad roof. . . .

For Paris emits limpid harmonies in the middle of the day : a cooing of pigeons, the sound of an aged piano. Ah! Here come the local picnickers—a young woman, one not so young, her mother, two small boys and a little girl. They are going to have lunch 'in the country'. All dressed up, wearing canvas shoes, laden with beach-bags, long French loaves, fruit and hard-boiled eggs, they march like conquerors across the Tuileries and settle down by the Orangery wall. For the Bois de Boulogne is too far away, five bus tickets. The other day, above their heads in the foliage, a little tawny owl rolled in a ball with its head sunk in its shoulders was painfully enduring the noontide. Its presence had been betrayed to me by a pool of white droppings on the ground. I kept his secret for him and one of the small picnickers was deceived : 'Look, someone has brought up his milk. . . .'

In the sleeping avenue de l'Opéra I press up against a window

to watch a dozen or so little seahorses swimming. The sight of
their up-and-down movements, their friendly excursions—they
go in pairs, one holding the other by the end of the tail—the
fluttering of their little dorsal rudders attracts no one else except
for a poor old creature laden with jewels. She tires of watching
before I do, murmuring as she departs : '*Milagros. . . .*'

The listlessness if not the leisure of August exerts great influence
over a quarter as old as the premier arrondissement. It leaves
intact those things that change but little over the centuries—
buildings, old men, children. A crippled concierge and his wheel-
chair emerge, secreted from an entrance-way, as if Balzac were
going to tell their story. Ferragus, chief of the devourers, may
have had one of his haunts at the top of this stairway winding
up to the black roof of a passage, glimpsed behind a shadowy
little girl seated on the lowest step. Threshold and child are both
greenish, and fragile in appearance. I can't help thinking of those
tiny flowers that grow on the damp sides of wells and are called
toad-flax. . . . The stairway is old, not inelegant, and clings to
the wall like an iron vine; a peeling notice announces that
diamonds are cut here. Until today the passers-by hid this from
me. They've also hidden that, in another house of the centre, the
bottom of the courtyard opens into another courtyard, beyond
which a wall in process of demolition looks down on an enclosed
garden. . . . Who owns this garden, the chestnut trees, the mossy
steps, the cat, the closed shutters? I do, to some extent, for everything is deserted, open, trusting, drowsy, the mason is on holiday,
the cat talks to me and a little red valerian allows itself to be
picked. To me also belongs everything that Paris produces and
displays and which, in a busier season, is beyond my reach or
my use, and that my self-respect prevents me from contemplating.
I am not far from getting interested in what is absolutely value-
less to me. How astonishing they are, these cages for breasts and
torso, the pink armour called a girdle whose upper part consists

of two glistening satin cones. And all the glassware, iron work, toys, imitation jade, imitation coral, imitation enamel, the thick polished stones, jewelled chokers, silver and gold bangles with glaucous swellings, isn't it all pretty? No, it's not always pretty. But these ornaments do possess the lure of icy gems, a submarine semi-transparency and refraction. Besides, they are here in such quantity. Certain shoe displays amount, in my barefoot estimation, almost to the level of temptation. The heels covered with material—oh dream, oh folly! And curling uppers! And strange things to clothe the feet—combinations of felt, cork, fishnet, rubber and cellophane!

To me again, and to you also, summer residents of Paris, belongs the rout of peaches that runs across the city, after the cherries have gone. Between eleven and one a furtive market in peaches is conducted along the pavements of the rue Saint-Honoré and its intersecting streets. You have to chase after it as the sellers are on the look-out for the police. But the peaches are worth the trouble this year, perfect under their fine velvet. What else is better value, or as beautiful, for fifty-five sous the pound? We August Parisians, who take the air on the quays and sun ourselves on the roofs, must not forget the varied and delicate gastronomy of Paris. It ranks among our just compensations and unlooked-for delights, competes with the pleasure of balconies at nightfall, the timely downpour, the comforts of a room arranged for rest and for work, the encounter with a familiar face rendered amiable by long absence. Let us be patient gracefully. Tomorrow, perhaps, a nostalgic odour of October will pass over our city—humid, premature, arriving by nocturnal steps after a sultry day. . . .

Provincial Paris

The removal men have gone. The ladder is folded up again. And my friends, climbing one by one the old stairway, beautiful now it's bare, dreaming one by one at the sight of the sun-filled mist that transforms the garden of the Palais-Royal this morning, say to me: 'Ah, so you are a provincial again?'

At which I assume the look of false modesty, the proud, upthrust chin of the collector. . . . Yes, I am a provincial again, in the Paris where the provinces exist, if not for everyone, at least for those who take the trouble to find them. Discover? Why not rediscover? The heart beats again. Forty-five years of Paris have not changed me from anything but a provincial, searching through twenty arrondissements and over both river banks for her lost homeland.

My last province but one goes back to the Champs-Elysées. Such a smart district must be barren territory for one who cultivates a particular mode of thought and regular habits, and drags along a suite of furniture obstinate in its mahogany and flowered dust-sheets and a constellation of massive, useless, brightly-coloured glassware. But my province was recreated from bits and pieces in the eighth arrondissement. A curtain hung over the barely-dry, too-white wall. A cordial atmosphere was created

146

between the toad-like armchair and the austere bookcase. When
the desk lamp was lit its circle of light embraced just the right
objects—older than I—and the proper souvenirs. To such an
extent, I had managed so well, that when the great wind of the
Parisian heights blew open my window, in May, it landed on my
blue page a wistaria flower, a yellow butterfly, a bee. For the
flora and fauna of Parisian balconies very obstinately refuse
to die out. When I was living at Claridge's in a province composed of a sloping slate roof, two narrow floral balconies and
two small rooms, all on the seventh floor, I saw in the deep
gutter, at different times, a peculiar, almost yellow, rat; a green
frog; an escaped monkey; and on holiday evenings I could see
below me, swimming in the illuminated air, the backs of night
birds.

Wistaria in tubs, red geraniums, crinkly mint and bee-balm,
thickets of new vines which change the reinforced concrete into
a convent wall—gracious, precarious province mocking a Parisian
captive, you were a part, and not the least part, of my sentimental
nourishment.

I'm so exacting. . . . If I can't have a tree-top under my eyes
I need a changing expanse of sky. Or else wild soaring wings. Or
else silence. Or else a hurrying human noise like the chattering
after leaving High Mass in a village. And the smell of warm
bread. And a voice thrown clear and sharp from a window over
the head of a little girl running. . . . I need to give a name to
familiar sights, even if I have to invent it. It happens miraculously,
in my sleep, that I confuse my well-loved provinces, my birthplace and others, and feel them gropingly if I wake up in
the middle of the night, to question the striking of some great
clock . . . I'm well aware, though, that it's in Provence—a
window-catch that exists only in memory, a bedside table
acquired in Brittany, a copper knob that gleamed half a century
ago on the door of my room as a child. . . . A smooth wall,

a rough-textured curtain, a glass of water, all gone, broken, exiled, are reborn when I return to myself. Meeting them again is as priceless and fleeting a moment as hoar-frost on a clear day, the only moment when I can put out my hand and almost touch the crumbling flower of the past, a gift granted by sensual memory, as inveterate in me as might be stammering or lameness. . . .

Yes, once more I've found a province in Paris. Each time I think it's the last. I like to think that I'll end up under the shade of some steeple, some old panelled ceiling, a colonnade, the remains of an arbour that used to shelter nuns. . . .

But the provinces are faithful only to those who know how to evoke them at the right moment. The same routine means a practised hand and entrenched habit. I acquired them long ago, these habits; you may find them rather ridiculous. Granted, I don't get them all from Sido, my mother, a disguised eccentric who kept to no rule. She was merely rustic, not provincial. The unforeseen in her life, which a village did nothing to narrow, happened by predilection, she grasped at it eagerly. What would she say to see me every morning? She'd say: 'Aren't you tired of that brown wool dress? And where do you go, every morning at the same time? You remind me of old Pimoulle, who used to visit his garden outside the village every day. It used to give me nervous palpitations to see him passing always at the same time. . . .'

I remember old Pimoulle very well. I knew him for seventeen years. I knew him when he was already old, older still, very old. My behaviour is much the same as his. Who has shaped me to such modest employment of my leisure, to the daily return to what's in store for me? I believe it's the provinces and their simple belief in habit as a votive force. . . . It's not that my snuggery always appeals to me—the table, the unfinished page, the lamp—or that it always gives me what I need from it. I'm less lucky, there, than the old man with his garden outside the walls. Each day, when he returned, he held in his mouth a sprig of violet, a sweet honeysuckle, a double cherry flower or, throughout the high season, a rose.

France, the Most
Beautiful Country in the World

In France, I cannot recall having consciously planned to visit a beauty-spot, a monument or a panorama. This one just happened to me, that one came my way, the other just opened before my eyes like the valleys we fly over in dreams. . . . Nevertheless, a malign fortune interposed to prevent me from visiting the towers of Merle and the chasm at Padirac.* After each failure I would begin again: 'It's all fixed, Pech-Merle today and Padirac tomorrow!' But on the way the car would shed a wheel or the horse a shoe, or perhaps some inn attracted us. Or else we ran across friends who led us astray: 'You've plenty of time! Merle and Padirac won't run away if you leave them!'

In the end I abandoned Padirac and Merle, which chance withheld from me but might yet restore. . . .

One of my friends, an Englishwoman, often remarks that we do not appreciate France sufficiently. She has settled among us after a globe-trotting career and has not stirred for thirty years, such is her love and admiration. She must be right. But what is the significance of her declaration for us French, who explore little and enjoy greatly? We are the spoilt children of a country worth all others. If our young people take to travelling in France they risk losing the sedentary habit that makes them lazy but clearsighted, cautious yet sensitive, absorbed in their own locality, their own riverside washing-place, their own lime-filled avenue, the horizons accessible to the traveller on foot. I recall a period when Frenchmen, though almost ignorant of their own country, made up for this with a complete, minute and lyrical acquaintance with their native parish. I am one of those stay-at-homes who can't stir ten leagues from their hearth without exclaiming in admiration. What do I know of France? A small part of Burgundy, some corners of Paris, two or three cantons of the Jura and Franche-Comté, expanses of tawny coast in Picardy and Brittany, the green meadows of Brives, the ruddy heath of the Plateau de Millevaches, and, finally, Provence—a small condensed Provence, so charming as to deprive me of any wish to go further. . . .

But did I ever experience a wish to go 'further'? Quite the contrary, I thought at first it would kill me. To leave my lakes with their rank odour of reeds and alders, their local mists, the secret springs that fed them—I pined for them for over a year when I was seventeen. But the Jura took over my cure, granted me the warmth of its days, the chill of its nights, the spark spurting under the nailed heel from its flinty skeleton. And the wild cyclamen taught me a new perfume. . . .

Not all my discoveries of the French countryside were so decisive or so passionate. Beside the sands at Crotoy I sulked like a girl someone marries against his will. I sought the sea, twenty kilometres out over the flat beaches, behind a mist that dulled the sun. . . . Four successive summers I returned alone to the grey sea, the racing tides with their rich phosphorescent flux, bringing shrimps and flatfish, crabs and sand-eels. When the turn of the tide coincided with sunset the far-off boats glided on a fiery red streak. . . .

I stopped crying for my lost new loves, I regained confidence.

Brittany bathed me in its blue milk, an atmospheric blue hung by the dawn from the branches of apple trees, from masts of boats and craggy rocks. How many times between waking and sleeping I chose to hear the curlews passing, crying in their nocturnal flight. . . .

Sometimes I long for a well-planned itinerary to put me down on the other side of the globe and bring me back again. A world tour is a short and definite trip. But to get to know France I trust to chance. It was chance, one 15th of July, that showered us with apricots and peaches the length of the Rhône valley. One village where we drank was all old gables, tiered roofs and children, another all flowers and fountains. I do not remember their names —what is the point? We shall find others even more beautiful. We are those French who are rather nonchalant, a little timid, but capable, nevertheless, of sitting quietly with something we appreciate. We bear a pleasantly drowsy love for France deep within us, fed, at each step, with delicate provender. *En route* we grumble sometimes, are sometimes optimistic. Without appearing to do so, we know better than anyone else that, round the bend of the road, at the street-corner, at the top of the slope, behind the hoardings and the hostelries, France keeps in bountiful reserve all she has that is mature and experienced, moving, unchanging and opulent. . . .

The immense sea, gliding calmly over a few square centimetres, a boundless sky. . . . An ancient tree, spring meadows, a low church. Tucked away in a declivity a Breton hamlet of brown thatch, tawny and bristly like a nest of hedgehogs; the forest with its deer, the snow, Provence in summer bleached by white fire, flat canals, angry waves, old Montmartre with its ruined gardens. . . .

One cannot contemplate this exhibition of 'French Landscapes' without a kind of blissful fatigue. It is unlike any other. Fellow-prisoners of Paris, go and immerse yourselves in contemplation of Cézanne's foliage, Daubigny's glacial majesty; delight in the four little Seurats, all sparkling water and sunshine, unless you prefer a honey-sweet Monticelli or the wall covered with narrow Corots as tall as the world. . . .

The lucid free piety that has gathered together here Rouart and Lépine, Segonzac and Georges Michel (who painted the parish church of Passy standing humbly in its jungle), has dispensed with the still life, the tyrannical bouquet and the malign gaze of portraits. The air of beaches comes to us from a dappled Boudin, a niche hewn in the cliffs from a Gauguin. A picture of Avallon restores the very smell of my birthplace, together with the recollection of an old gentleman with a red nose whom I met in the local train. He was going to buy cakes at Saint-Fargeau and was named Harpignies. . . .

How beautiful they are, these pure and humane landscapes! And an even greater contentment rewards my ignorance of painting. I shall never know, nor wish to know, 'how it is done' —for instance, that impalpable, perfect and mysterious replica of breathable air that bathes and intersperses the branches of Cézanne's green tree. Nor why I enjoy, at the other extreme, that canvas where everything is spiny, hostile, burnt with dust— Van Gogh's 'Thistles'. Nor why, though indifferent to Matisse's designs, I am overwhelmed by these 'Trees' spread against a silver sky.

Monet's flowered hayfield, the Bonnard rich in vegetation and colour, an enchantingly precise Derain, the sinewy curve that Segonzac gives his vigorous tree-trunks, a small Leprin that surpasses a large Utrillo—I find everything here intelligible, wholesome, surprising yet familiar.

It's because all that decorates these walls is French and celebrates the landscapes of France. Dead or alive, the painters collected at the Galérie Charpentier worked with a patient and loving hand, travelled leisurely, for the most part rarely left their barge, their meadow, their terrace. One may have escaped to paint Tahiti; the others stayed faithful, rooted and unmoving.

A poet friend exclaimed : 'Take me when I'm asleep, put me down among these canvases, and I'll wake up and cry "This is France!"'

In this lyricism dwells part of the truth. In matters concerning France we are all poets in our different ways. But the privileged painter of landscape has the joy and honour to hand on to us, in Nature's unchanging shape, the precious image of what is only transient, by reason of light, reflection and cloud. He does not pursue his 'subject', he awaits it. Even though he stirs no further than from his threshold to his own field, he is like the true traveller who journeys and halts frequently. In France the painter hardly needs to evoke the eloquence of a site or a panorama. Our landscape painters are enamoured of dreaming spires, riverside washing-places, a balanced beauty that seems a perpetual challenge to their art. In this exhibition we can breathe deeply the atmosphere created by an enlightened cult. It is a healthy one and revives within us the pride in those inestimable gifts that peace and prosperity make us forget. Happiness teaches us little about love; we become sure of it, and its strength, only through suffering. Look at the rich fields of a country torn in two; here are the harvests, the waves, the apple trees in blossom. Here are the beautiful features of the countryside of France, warm from having cradled, nourished and buried a human being in every fold.

Notes

Three . . . Six . . . Nine . . .

[1] Marguerite Moreno (1871–1948), was a close friend of Colette and is mentioned in several of her books. Colette's letters to her have also been published. One of her most famous creations was the title role in Giraudoux's *The Madwoman of Chaillot* (1945).

[2] Augustin Pajou (1730–1809), was a prolific sculptor who won the Prix de Rome in 1748 and later became a member of the Académie.

[3] Adrienne Lecouvreur (1692–1730), the actress, lived in the narrow rue Visconti, which backed on to the rue Jacob. She was the mistress of the Maréchal de Saxe, and was probably poisoned by a jealous rival. The house was later occupied by the symbolist critic Remy de Gourmont, author of *Letters to the Amazon*, addressed to Natalie Clifford Barney.

[4] Prosper Mérimée (1803–70), famous as the author of *Carmen*, lived at 18 rue Jacob in 1848.

[5] José-Maria de Heredia (1842–1905), was the Parnassian poet, born in Cuba, of half Spanish origin.

[6] Renée Vivien was an English Lesbian poet, whose real name was Pauline Tarn. Colette wrote a striking account of her in *The Pure and the Impure*.

[7] Arthème Fayard (1866–1936), the son of the founder of the well-known publishing firm.

[8] Polaire was an actress and music-hall star of Algerian origin, a friend of Colette when they were both young. Cocteau sketched them together and said of Polaire that she was 'as violent as a yiddish insult and stood poised at the edge of the skating-rink like a fit of hysterics'.

[9] La Grande Mademoiselle (1627–93), was the Duchesse de Montpensier, and a niece of Louis XIII. She is remembered for her support of Condé during the Fronde, her unhappy love-affair with Lauzun and her lively *Memoirs*.

[10] Colette de Jouvenel, the daughter of Colette and Henri de Jouvenel, was born in 1913. Colette met Henri de Jouvenel, editor of *Le Matin*, while she was contributing regularly to that paper.

[11] Eve Lavallière (1866–1929), achieved great success in plays by Croisset and other popular dramatists.

[12] La Canebière is an important avenue in Marseilles leading to the port.

[13] Alexandre Stavisky (1886–1934), was of Russian origin, and organized one of the biggest financial swindles of the thirties.

[14] Edouard Detaille (1848–1912), was a painter who specialized in military subjects.

Maiden Voyage of the Normandie

* Colette and Maurice Goudeket were married in 1935, two months before the maiden voyage of the *Normandie*.

Morocco

* Marshal Lyautey (1854–1934), helped to establish the French protectorate in Morocco and became the first Resident General (1912–25).

In Burgundy

[1] *marque*. This is a reference to the name under which an individual wine is marketed, guaranteeing its type and quality.

[2] *cru*. This could be roughly translated as 'growth'. The French usage denotes a vineyard or group of vineyards producing wine of uniformly high quality suitable for independent recognition under the laws governing the classification of vineyards and their products.

My Poor Burgundy

[1] *setier*. This was an ancient measure which varied according to the district and the material measured. The liquid *setier* was equivalent to about a gallon.

[2] *verriné*. An obsolete word referring to a glassful.

Le Désert de Retz

[1] Le Désert de Retz is situated near Chambourcy, at the edge of the forest of Marly, some twenty kilometres from Paris. In the late eighteenth century these grounds were bought by Monsieur de Monville who built a group of 'follies', including a temple to Pan, a Chinese pavilion and the house in the shape of a truncated column described here.

[2] pomegranates.

An Earthly Paradise

[1] Clères. The district capital of the Seine-Inférieure. All the animals in its private zoo are at large.

[2] Colette wrote the libretto for Ravel's opera *L'enfant et les sortilèges* during the First World War. The staging of the first production in 1925 was criticized, much to the disappointment of the composer. The work has since been accepted as a masterpiece.

La Treille Muscate I

* This house near St Tropez was originally called Tamaris-les-Pins and renamed by Colette. She sold it in 1938 because the district had become overcrowded in summer.

France, the Most Beautiful Country in the World

* The chasm at Padirac, with its underground river, is a famous tourist site in the Dordogne. The caves at Pech-Merle in the same area, famous for their prehistoric paintings, were discovered in 1922.

PQ2605
.028
A254
1971

Colette, Sidonie
    Gabrielle

    Places